WITHDRAWN

LILITH'S ARK

This book was made possible
through a generous grant by
The Lowell and Harriet Glazer
Family Foundation

LILITH'S ARK
Teenage Tales of Biblical Women

Deborah Bodin Cohen

2006 • 5766
THE JEWISH PUBLICATION SOCIETY
Philadelphia

The Jewish Publication Society
2100 Arch Street
Philadelphia, PA 19103
www.jewishpub.org

Manufactured in the United States of America
    06 07 08 09 10 10 9 8 7 6 5 4 3 2 1

Library of Congress Cataloging-in-Publication Data
    Cohen, Deborah Bodin, 1968-
    Lilith's ark : teenage tales of biblical women / Deborah Bodin Cohen.
        p. cm.
    ISBN 0-8276-0833-0 (alk. paper)
    1. Women in the Bible—Fiction. 2. Teenage girls—Fiction. I. Title.
    PS3603.O344L55 2006
    813'.6—dc22

                                                                2006005252

Book design and typesetting by Jonathan Kremer

To David, my devoted husband

Contents

Acknowledgments

Lilith's Ark began as a final project in a modern *midrash* class taught by Dr. Norman Cohen at Hebrew Union College-Jewish Institute of Religion in New York. Several fellow students, now rabbinic colleagues, encouraged me to expand my short project into a book. I thank my colleagues in the rabbinic class of 1997 for this initial impetus. Years later, when I found time to write, I remembered their enthusiasm.

The staff members at The Jewish Publication Society were my dedicated partners in preparing *Lilith's Ark* for publication. I thank Dr. Rena Potok for her thoughtful comments, invaluable critiques, and belief in this book's potential. I thank Emily Law for her careful editing and her insightful feedback. I thank Carol Hupping, Janet Liss, and Robin Norman for their dedication in seeing *Lilith's Ark* through production and Arielle Levites for her enthusiasm in publicizing the book.

I am blessed with many friends who volunteered to read the manuscript at various stages. I thank Kelly Fineman and Julie Winkler for their thorough attention and constructive suggestions. Kendall Berry, Jeanie Blanton, Dr. Loren Firstenberg, and Julie Weitzman volunteered to be a mock book club. Their suggested questions and themes helped immensely in writing the book's discussion guide.

My colleagues at Temple Emanuel in Cherry Hill, N.J., assisted and encouraged me throughout this project. In particular, I thank Rabbi Jerome P. David, Rabbi Geri Newburge, Mayda Clarke, and Barry Pisetzner for their constant support and Jean Klein and Andrea Miller for their able administrative help.

I gleaned much of my information about life during biblical times from two sources: *Everyday Life in Bible Times*, 3rd edition, by Arthur W. Klinck and Erich H. Keihl and *Daily Life in Biblical Times* by Oded Borowski.

Often when writing I thought about my own young daughter, Arianna. Knowing that one day she would read *Lilith's Ark* provided much inspiration. I look forward to passing *Lilith's Ark* on to her someday and witnessing her gifts develop.

Introduction

Imagine that you are holding a small wooden box. A craftswoman has lovingly carved intricate designs into the box's lid. The carvings reveal two figures— a woman and a man, or perhaps a teenage girl and a boy, or two best friends— holding hands in a lush garden. When you open the box, girls' voices call out, asking you to listen to their stories and learn from them. You hear Sarah laugh, Rebekah pray, Rachel argue with Leah, Dinah cry. Inside the box, you see everyday items such as a map, a mirror, and a blanket. You know that these items are precious. Each item represents the story of a woman in the Torah when she was young. You are holding Lilith's ark.

I invite you to open Lilith's ark and hear stories of the Torah's women, as I envision them during their teen years and beyond. *Lilith's Ark* is a *midrash*, a story that grows from the Torah text and the imagination. From the time of the first rabbis over 2,000 years ago, Jews have written *midrashim*. These rabbis of the talmudic era taught that each verse, each phrase, each word of the Torah hints at new stories waiting to be discovered. Every reader of the Torah can create *midrash* by reading the Bible sensitively, looking for hints of stories beyond the story and relying on her own imagination and experiences. Just as I have created *midrashim*, so can you.

Imagine now that you are opening the Torah ark in a synagogue. You are holding a Torah scroll. Feel its weight. Sense the beauty of its words, the eternal lessons it holds. For all that the Torah teaches, it provides sparse details about biblical women and tells us even less about these women's teen years. The women of Torah grew up at a time very different from ours, a time when women's and men's roles were rigidly defined and girls married early, often to relatives as close as uncles or first cousins. The concept of being a "teenager" did not exist during the biblical era. Childhood led directly into adulthood with little time for the exploration that marks the "teenage" years today. As the women of the Torah matured through their teen years, the ages of 13 to 19, they did not have the time or freedom to be teenagers.

Although their world was dramatically different, these young biblical women faced challenges essentially the same as the ones teenagers face today. We find hints of these women's first loves, blossoming spirituality, and developing bodies and identities in the Torah. From the hints that I found, I created *midrashim* about the teen years of 10 women in Genesis and how these years affected their lives. I melded the Torah text, later biblical commentaries, and historic details about the ancient world with my own experiences, the experiences of girls and women whom I know, and my imagination. Envisioning a Torah ark, I imagined Lilith's ark holding these women's stories.

I am not alone in creating *midrashim* of the Torah's women. From the time Jews first read from Torah, Jewish women undoubtedly found hints of untold women's stories in the text and elaborated on them. Unfortunately, these women's *midrashim* were never written down and have been forgotten. We are lucky to live at a time when women's stories are valued and shared. During the past generation, many Jewish women have been inspired to write and publish beautiful and meaningful *midrashim*. *Lilith's Ark* is unique because it is written for you—today's Jewish teenager. I hope that *Lilith's Ark* will inspire you to seek out other *midrashim* and, perhaps, to create such stories of your own. *Lilith's Ark* is my gift to you, a reader of the next generation.

Prologue

LILITH: A HOLY ARK

A HINT FROM TORAH:

And God created man in His image, in the image of God He created him; male and female He created them. GENESIS 1:27–28

The book of Genesis includes two versions of how God created woman and man. In the first chapter of Genesis, God creates woman and man together. In the second chapter, God creates Adam and takes one of his ribs to create Eve. The ancient rabbis, questioning what happened to the first woman, created fanciful *midrashim* about her. They named her Lilith after a demon in ancient Middle Eastern mythology whose name means "night spirit." In their *midrashim*, Lilith considers herself Adam's equal partner, since God created them together. But Adam expects her to be subservient. Lilith protests by leaving Adam and the Garden of Eden. She becomes a demon and roams the world at night, seducing teenage boys and men in their dreams. In the last several decades, Jewish woman have reclaimed Lilith, portraying her as a heroine for demanding equality.

Let us meet Lilith...

Now, you see me.

Now, you don't.

Look for me in the Torah, if you wonder whether I exist.

Am I mist?

Or a story twist?

You see my shadow. You hear my voice.

Is it you? Or is it me?

Let's see…I'm a mystery.

So maybe you should just let me be.

Some say I am a temptress of teenage boys, visiting their steamy dreams.

Others call me the first feminist, whatever that means.

Strong-minded, self-assured, sensitive, secretive, supportive, suave, saucy, sassy, sexy, sweet.

I am a little bit of each.

I am sugar, I am spice.

I am naughty, I am nice.

Smell me in lilacs and lilies, their perfume a delight.

Sense me in the *lailah*—in the darkest night.

At my secrets, I will allow you to peek.

It is teenage girls, not boys, whom I seek.

I whisper in their ears as they sleep, "You are God's image. You can become your dreams. You are beautiful and powerful, creative and smart, witty and perceptive."

Sometimes they wake and listen, sometimes they just continue to sleep.

If rhymes and chimes confuse you, let me tell it to you straight. I am the first woman. You heard me right. I came first, then Eve. They call me Lilith. Since you asked, I prefer the name Bezalelit—in God's image. Some claim that I was forced out of Eden because I dared to argue with my husband. Let them believe that story, if they want. Adam was good-natured and kind, but no match for me. I much prefer to think that I left Eden because I was too smart. I knew too much. I challenged God. And, I loved apples.

Created in God's image, I began prophesying the future early. On the first Shabbat, I munched on an apple from the Tree of Knowledge. The power of the Tree of Knowledge was certainly strong. That night, I dreamt of Sarah and Abraham, who lived generations after me. The next week, I sat under the Tree and images of their son, Isaac, and his wife, Rebekah, came to me. Soon I pulled a branch off the Tree of Knowledge and chiseled it into a pen. Using ink from berries, I began to write down their stories.

On the 40th night, I climbed to the top of the Tree of Knowledge because I had eaten all the fruit off the lower branches. As I pulled down an apple from a high branch, I foresaw the artist Bezalel, who lived at the time of Miriam and Moses. I watched him build the Holy Ark to carry God's words in the desert after the Israelites left Egypt. Eating my second apple, I saw Moses, Miriam, and Aaron putting the tablets of the Ten Commandments in the Holy Ark. The very next morning, I began carving a small ark for myself.

God called out, "Young lady, what are you doing? Bezalel doesn't build the Holy Ark until Exodus 35."

Apple in hand, I replied, "I am Bezalelit, created in the divine image. I am making a Holy Ark to hold my prophecies."

God said, "You are moving too quickly, little girl. I just created you and now you think that you are all grown up. You cannot do everything that you want. I forbid you to eat from the Tree of Knowledge."

God was not ready for a smart aleck girl like me. I left the garden and went out on my own. Soon I began to fade from everybody's memory.

Do I exist?

Am I just mist or a story twist?

Since nobody knows my true history, why not enjoy being a mystery?

One more secret I will share.

I hid something in Eden, just a hint that I was there.

I left my ark behind for future girls and women to find.

Now you see me.

Now you don't.

Abracadabra is Hebrew, did you know?

It means, "If it is spoken, it comes to be."

Maybe, if you say my name—LILITH—you can make me be.

1 EVE: THE SEEDS OF AN APPLE

A HINT FROM TORAH:

And the Lord God fashioned the rib that He had taken from the man into a woman; and He brought her to the man. GENESIS 2:22

Eve is the first woman named in the Torah. Her name appropriately means "life," since she is the mother of all future generations. God creates her to be Adam's companion and helper in the Garden of Eden. They have immature knowledge, not even realizing that they are naked. Eve is the first person to disobey God. God forbids Eve and Adam to eat from the Tree of Knowledge of Good and Evil. But a serpent convinces Eve to eat from this tree and she, in turn, gives its fruit to Adam to eat. According to popular belief, Eve eats an apple, although Jewish tradition also describes the fruit as grapes, figs, or citrons. Because Eve and Adam eat from the Tree of Knowledge, God banishes them from the Garden of Eden. Eve's motivation for disobeying God has been debated throughout the generations. Was she simply duped by the serpent, or did she choose to pursue knowledge regardless of its price?

Let us meet Eve...

I remember the moment of my birth. I awoke to the sensation of moisture. Thick dew covered my body. Crusty pus stuck my eyelids together. I heard a deep moaning. As I struggled to blink, I clawed at the thick moss of my birth bed. My eyelids separated. A landscape of muted greens replaced the bloodred darkness of my closed eyes. Slowly, my eyes focused. Tall trees with jagged bark and lush leaves appeared. Small crimson and lavender flowers blossomed among ferns. Owls peered down curiously at me from sycamore trees. The serpent rubbed against me, then crept away on its short legs.

I rolled onto my side. A few arms' lengths away, a boy lay in the moss, his knees pulled up to his chin. A thin, bloody wound cut from his chest to his back. He moaned again. I lifted my body and crawled to the boy. When I touched his back, the wound healed itself, turning brown then pale pink before disappearing. The boy turned to me.

"Are you my helper?" said the boy. "I call myself Adam."

"Are you my friend?" I replied.

He looked up through the canopy of leaves to the sky and called out, "At last, this one is bone of my bones and flesh of my flesh."

Monkeys snickered and swung through the trees.

Holding a tree trunk for support, I lifted my body. My legs felt weak beneath me, and I struggled not to fall.

Adam said, "I will show you my garden. I call it Eden."

Together, Adam and I walked through the dense ferns and grasses until a path appeared. Ahead of us, gazelles roamed; overhead, I saw hawks soaring.

Adam said, "I till and tend the garden. The work is not difficult. God does not wish for us to toil."

Adam brought me to a vineyard. He plucked a juicy purple grape from a vine and handed it to me. I put it into my mouth and tasted its sweetness. We moved from vineyard to orchard. I ate pomegranates, olives, and dates. I savored my first sensations of taste. The serpent passed us and crept toward the center of the garden. I began to follow.

"Stay with me," insisted Adam. "We do not go into the garden's center."

"Why not?" I asked.

"God has spoken. The Tree of Knowledge of Good and Evil grows there," Adam warned. "If we eat its fruit—or even touch it—we will die."

I heeded Adam's warning, fighting my own curiosity to explore. As the sun began to fall, Adam and I climbed a rocky path. At dusk, we arrived at a dark cave on the edge of a cliff.

"This is my home," Adam said. "And now, your home as well."

I sat on the cliff's edge. The brilliant oranges, reds, and pinks of the setting sun delighted me.

"Come, sit with me," I called out to Adam. He came and stood over me.

"Do not worry," he said. "I also feared my first setting sun. I believed that the sun would disappear forever. But each morning, it rises."

Adam had mistaken my exhilaration for alarm.

"I do not fear," I replied.

That night as we lay on our mats, the sounds of crickets filled the air. In the distance, I heard a coyote howl.

"Does the darkness scare you?" Adam whispered.

"The animals sing to us their lullaby," I answered, to soothe him.

In the morning, I awoke before Adam. Quietly, I left our cave and began to climb. Nearby, I found a lookout from which I could see all of Eden. A mighty river ran over rapids, cutting through the garden's center. As its currents flowed out of Eden, it separated into four smaller rivers. I wondered where each river led. I saw tan desert, orange canyon, and green oasis in the distance. I imagined exploring those distant lands. When I returned to the cave, I found Adam standing at its dark entrance, his arms crossed.

"Why did you leave?" he said. "You made me worry. You are young and have only begun to learn your way."

"I wanted to explore," I replied simply, not understanding the reason for his concern. "I saw the rivers. Do you know what lies beyond them?"

"I neither wonder nor ask," Adam answered. "I know enough to live within Eden, and I do not need to know more. Come with me. We must gather nuts and fruit to eat."

Adam and I wandered back to the vineyard and orchard. Goats and deer sniffed me curiously. The serpent circled my feet and hissed. I was certain that the serpent mouthed the word "come" before creeping toward the garden's center.

"Let us return to the cave," said Adam, his gaze following the serpent.

"You go without me," I answered. "I want to pick a few more olives and dates." Adam started to protest.

"I will be fine," I insisted.

I waited until I could no longer see Adam. Then I followed the path of the serpent. I had taken only a few steps when I heard a hiss.

"I listened to your questions," rasped the serpent. "The rivers are named the Pishon, Gihon, Tigris, and Euphrates. The Pishon leads to a land of gold, onyx, and gemstones."

I saw only the serpent's tail as it darted under a branch and disappeared. I chased after it and found myself in a marshy bog surrounded by tall bulrush. Insects landed on my neck. As I leaned down to swat a dragonfly off my ankle, I saw something protruding from a hollow log. I reached inside the log and felt an object lodged against the wood. I grasped it, then pulled hard. Out came a wooden box, covered with mud and spiderwebs. I ran my hand over the box's lid to clean off the grime. The box was beautiful, with scenes of the garden around me carved out of the wood. On the lid, a man and woman faced one another, arms outstretched. I opened the box. It was empty.

I heard a rustle behind me. The serpent reappeared, creeping over the log.

"You found it. Very good," said the serpent. "That box is called an ark."

"Who made it?" I asked. "What should I do with it?"

The serpent just smiled, turned around, and crawled away.

Carefully, I put the ark under my arm and climbed back to the cave. When I showed the ark to Adam, I sensed that he had seen it before.

"Do you know who made this ark?" I asked.

Adam mumbled a name that sounded liked "lily." Then he looked at me and said, "I do not know."

"Perhaps God carved it and placed it in the garden for me to find," I said. "I need to learn the ark's purpose."

Adam asked, "Why would God have left this ark for you and not for me?"

The next morning, I again helped Adam harvest fruit from the orchard and vineyard. When we had picked our fill, I asked Adam to explore the garden with me. He refused.

"I wish to return to the cave," Adam said. I sensed urgency in his voice.

"I suppose the animals could be my fellow explorers," I replied.

I turned from Adam and began to walk. A gust of wind pushed me toward Eden's center. I felt smooth skin circle my ankles.

"Look upward," hissed the serpent. "Those magnificent branches grow

from the Tree of Life. The branches cover all of Eden like a mother bird protecting her young under her wings. It grows next to the Tree of Knowledge.
Come, let me show you its beauty up close."

"I cannot go," I said without conviction.

"You can go," the serpent said. "You simply wish to avoid the unknown."

The serpent crept into a hedge of myrtle bushes and vanished under their
camouflage. I heard a rustle, and then nothing. I waited, but the serpent did not
reappear. I considered following the serpent into the bushes, but I feared getting lost in the thick, tall foliage. Instead, I started to climb back to the cave.
From my lookout, I might see the Tree of Life and its embracing branches.
Perhaps I could even glimpse the Tree of Knowledge.

As I walked, I felt a breeze. The breeze became a wind that blew with
increasing strength. My hair flew into my face, and my body felt chilled.
Pushing my hair aside, I beheld the most curious sight. Adam sat on a stone cliff,
his face pressed into the wind. He was speaking loudly.

"You said that You would make a fitting helper for me," Adam said to
the wind.

"Adam," I called out. "To whom do you speak?"

The wind immediately stopped.

"You startled me," Adam said, sitting up stiffly.

"To whom do you speak?" I repeated.

"You may be too young to understand," Adam said. "I will try to explain.
Each afternoon, I hurry back to our cave to speak to God. God wishes to record
our story in a scroll called the Torah."

"Should I not also speak to God?" I asked. "Surely, God wishes to hear
from me as well."

"God created me first," Adam said. "You were created to be my helper.
Can I not speak for both of us?"

"I wish to tell my own story," I said.

I felt the emotion of anger for the first time. I bit my lip and felt my
cheeks turn red. I did not know how to react. Then I felt a slight breeze on my
legs, which cooled my emotions and allowed me to think. I knew what I had
to do. I turned from Adam. Without speaking, I began to run.

I found the serpent's path and rushed toward the Tree of Knowledge.
Peacocks, rams, and leopards stopped, raised their heads, and watched me pass.

Soon, a mammoth tree trunk stood in front of me. The Tree of Life. I climbed over its network of protruding roots, careful not to fall. Behind the Tree of Life, I saw a field of thick, rich grass. The Tree of Knowledge grew in the center of the field. Sunlight sparkled off its emerald green leaves and ebony black trunk. Fruit as bright as rubies hung from the tree's branches. The serpent lay on a low branch, watching me.

"You chose knowledge," the serpent said. "As soon as you eat its fruit, you will understand both good and bad."

"The fruit looks good for eating, and it is a delight to the eye," I said, building my resolve. "I desire its wisdom."

I tugged hard on a piece of the tree's sparkling red fruit. The fruit broke off into my hand. I felt heat move from my fingers through my body. I lifted it up, gazed at its beauty, and bit. Sweet juice filled my mouth. My tongue and throat grew hot. I began to perspire. I felt my body grow and change. I developed curves, a thinner waist, and round breasts. I lifted my hands to my face. High cheekbones of womanhood had replaced the full face of a child. I looked down and realized that I was nude. The serpent smirked at me, and I blushed. I ran behind a fig tree and covered my body with its leaves. Then I felt desire. I wanted a companion, a man, with whom I could explore the world. I returned to the Tree of Knowledge and plucked a second piece of fruit from its branches.

Out of breath, I ran to Adam. His jaw dropped when he saw me.

"I am now a woman," I said to him. "And you are just a boy. Eat the fruit, and we will become equals. If you refuse, I will call out to God and tell my story without you."

Adam hesitated.

"Do not fear," I said. "Knowledge is good."

Adam bit into the fruit, gagging on its heat. His chest grew wide and hairy, his arms thick and strong, and his face angular and handsome. I felt my body drawn to him. I ran to Adam and gave him fig leaves to cover himself. We felt a breeze and heard the leaves rustle.

"Come, let us hide before God discovers what we have done," Adam said, grabbing my hand.

We ran to the orchard and hid among the trees. I clung to Adam, and he kissed me. We laughed. I looked up and saw the serpent grinning from a tree.

I glared at the serpent. I pulled Adam farther into the orchard, away from the serpent's view. We felt the wind again.

"Where are you?" called God.

Adam began to shake. He whispered, "I was afraid because I was naked, so I hid."

"Who told you that you were naked? Did you eat of the tree from which I had forbidden you to eat?" cried God.

Adam looked at me with anger mixed with desire.

"The woman You put at my side—she gave me the fruit and I ate," he said apologetically.

I felt fear for the first time.

"What is this you have done!" roared God.

"The serpent duped me, and I ate," I responded weakly, immediately regretting my answer. I desired knowledge, but feared telling God.

The serpent frowned at my betrayal.

God said to the serpent, "Because you did this, on your belly shall you crawl and dirt shall you eat all the days of your life."

The serpent fell from the tree. When it reached the ground, I saw that it no longer had legs. The serpent slithered toward me, brushed against my heel, and vanished into a grove of reeds. I clung to Adam.

Then God spoke to me. "I will make most severe your pangs in childbearing."

Adam held me close and kissed my forehead to console me. I smiled.

"Adam, I heard you moan after God plucked your rib and formed me. I saw your bloody wound," I said. "I can accept the pain, for God will form children from my body. I, too, will create life."

Finally, God spoke to Adam. "By toil, you shall eat all the days of your life. By the sweat of your brow shall you get bread to eat, until you return to the ground—For dust you are and to dust you shall return."

Adam and I looked at each other silently. The sun began to set.

Adam sighed, reached for my hand, and spoke. "I will call you Eve, for it means life. You will be the mother of all the living."

Before darkness fell on Eden, God banished us beyond the garden's gates. As the wind pushed us out of Eden, I clung to the ark that I had found in the log. I opened its lid and placed seeds from the Tree of Knowledge inside it.

Small and brown and dry, the seeds held great mystery, a life contained within their shell. I knew not what lay ahead of me; life was a mystery for me to explore and discover.

Our life outside the garden began. We had children, who brought us great joy and great pain.

When my hair turned white and my face wrinkled, I gave the ark to my son Seth's wife, and she in turn passed it down to the next generation of women. Each woman who received the ark placed a precious object into it before giving it to her daughter, sister, niece, or friend.

Every object, like my seeds, had a story. The tradition of passing down the ark continued.

Now the ark has been passed to you. Hold it in your hands. Open our ark, take out our gifts to you, listen to our stories, and try to know us. You can even add your own gift and your own story.

2 | SARAH: THE MAP

A HINT FROM TORAH:

Sarah said, "God has brought me laughter; everyone who hears will laugh with me." GENESIS 21:6

Sarah, the first matriarch and Abraham's wife, grows up in Babylonia, near where the Euphrates River empties into the Persian Gulf. Her parents gave her the name Sarai, but God changes her name to Sarah, which means "princess." God commands Abraham to leave their homeland, promising a new land for his descendants. Abraham takes Sarah and they journey throughout the Near East with an ever-growing camp of religious followers and servants. When Sarah remains barren into her elder years, she gives her servant Hagar to Abraham so they may have a child. Then, the unexpected happens. Three angels, disguised as travelers, visit the elderly Sarah and Abraham and announce that she will have a child. A year later, Sarah gives birth. She names her son Isaac, which means "laughter."

Let us meet Sarah...

I remember my palm tree, its long spines of branches fanning out shade. I would sit with my back up against its trunk, my legs dangling toward the cool water of the Euphrates River below. From my perch, I laughed as my younger sisters and cousins kicked the water and jumped like lizards from one rock to the next. Downriver, in the city of Ur, children could not play in the water. There, the river flowed so quickly that boats with colorful sails rode its currents. I preferred the quiet of the river near my home.

When I was a child, I too splashed and laughed in the river. My older cousin Milcah had sat, her back against the palm tree, and watched over me. Since I was the next eldest, I sometimes sat with Milcah. She told me every detail of her upcoming wedding. I envied Milcah for knowing her future. Since birth, Milcah had been promised to Nahor, her father's younger brother. Milcah confided that during her last visit to Ur, she had let Nahor kiss her. The next rainy season, she married Nahor and moved to Ur.

"Sarai," my mother said, "You are the eldest now. It is your duty to take Milcah's place and watch over the children as they play in the river."

Each morning, I helped my mother grind wheat. Each afternoon, I fed the sheep and spun their fleece into yarn. My mother told me stories and we laughed as we worked. In the late afternoons, when my mother and I saw the sun move toward the west, I brought the children down to the river. Tucking my tunic up under my belt, I waded into the water and rinsed the dust from my face. The children jumped like falling spindles into the river, spraying water over me. In jest, I scolded them and climbed out of the river. Then I sat under my palm tree, closed my eyes, and listened to the children's laughter echo in the river canyon.

I daydreamed of raising my own children by the river's edge. But I knew that there were no eligible boys in our small village. Like Milcah, I would leave my parents and marry a boy from Ur. As my body slowly changed, I worried about my future. My breasts grew larger, first to the size of olives, then apricots, and then small onions. With each new moon, my legs grew longer and, as I sat against the palm tree, they hung closer to the river. When the soles of my feet began to touch the water, I knew that soon I would marry.

My parents counted my birthday by the wheat harvest, for I was born in the late spring. Fourteen harvests had passed since my birth. After each harvest, my father loaded his donkey with grain and journeyed to the market in Ur. When I was younger and had fewer chores at home, I went with my father to Ur. We celebrated my birthday by eating pomegranates or sweet dates in the market. Now, my father went alone. I missed our time together, just the two of us. I watched the children play in the river and waited for my father's return. My mother, aunt, and I were eager for news of Milcah.

"Milcah gave birth to a second child, another healthy boy. Nahor named the baby Buz," my father announced as soon as he returned. "Nahor's father, Terah, says that our village water has made Milcah as strong as an ox and fertile as a young ewe. He wishes to find as good a wife for his younger son, Abram. He asked many questions about our Sarai."

Not even one moon passed before Terah visited our village. He said that he came to purchase more wheat from my father, but he appeared much more interested in me. I tried not to be self-conscious, but I blushed as Terah watched me do my daily tasks. He tasted the bread that I baked and asked for more. Terah smiled when I took the children to the river, stopping with my two youngest cousins to examine an empty bird's nest.

"The chicks must have grown up and left home," I explained to the children. "I wonder how far away they flew."

One of my cousins found a toppled grapevine and all the children grabbed for its fruit. Terah laughed when I halfheartedly disciplined the children.

"Stop acting like locusts," I scolded, taking a few grapes for myself.

"See, Sarai loves children. Look how she manages eight children at one time," my father told Terah. "She dreams of raising many sons and daughters."

At the next new moon, Terah returned and brought Abram with him. Abram walked with confidence and had a boyish face. He bowed slightly when he saw me. Although I pretended to look away, I saw that his arms were muscular and lean. He had black curls that grazed his shoulders. Abram knelt before my father and presented him with an idol for prosperity.

Earlier in the day, my mother had taken me to the river to bathe my body and wash my hair. She gently combed my auburn hair and braided it. For the first time, I wore makeup—blue kohl around my eyes, and cinnamon perfume on my neck.

"Just a little color and a drop of perfume are best," my mother told me. "Let a boy see your beauty, the way the gods intended you to look."

We spent two days preparing a feast, filling our best clay bowls with breads, cucumbers, melon, and lentil stew. Even though my family rarely ate meat, we boiled veal spiced with coriander. The men and boys sat on straw mats. I took Abram's plate and placed a portion of each food on it. He tasted the veal and smiled softly. Then, he looked at Terah and nodded. Reaching up, Terah placed a bronze bracelet on my arm, marking my betrothal to Abram. My time for marriage had come.

In the days before our wedding, I worked next to my mother and she shared the secrets of being a wife.

"Remember your role as wife, Sarai," my mother counseled. "Share your opinions with Abram, but when he makes a decision, you must support him. A husband takes charge. Abram is an ambitious and kind man. You have done well."

I dreaded leaving my village home, but knew it must be done. I sat against my palm tree and watched the children play. I closed my eyes and tried to etch the sound of the children's laughter into my mind. In Ur, the river with its boats and sailors was so loud that it drowned out all other sounds around it. People tied their donkeys to the palm trees by the river. Donkey dung made it impossible to sit under the palms.

Terah defied tradition and allowed us to be married in my village. Usually, a couple wed at the groom's home, but I desired more than anything for my mother to attend. Abram and I were married in a small grove of palms. I could hear the river gurgle and giggle in the background. After the wedding, the children played in the river. My next oldest cousin, Iscah, leaned against my palm tree and watched over them. My mother pulled me aside and gave me a stone container of eye makeup and a glass vial of perfume. Then she gave me an asherah, a fertility idol shaped like a goddess.

"When you give birth to your first child, I will visit you in Ur," she said as she hugged me good-bye.

My father tied my belongings to his donkey. Terah, Abram, my father, and I walked by the river for a day and a half until we reached Ur. As soon as we walked through the city's gates, I saw the ziggurat, a giant pyramid built in tiers, rising in front of us. A temple to the gods stood at the top of the ziggurat. Just past the ziggurat, the mud-brick homes of Ur rose up a gentle hill. Men and women walked quickly through the dusty alleys, some balancing water jugs on their heads and others shepherding small herds of goats. Abram and Terah pointed toward their store, down in the market. Terah sculpted idols from clay. Abram sold the idols to townsfolk.

We walked through the alleys until I could no longer hear the river. We arrived at a small house. Milcah greeted me at the doorway, holding an infant. A little boy peered out from behind her tunic and giggled.

Milcah leaned down and spoke to the boy, "I want you to meet Sarai. She is my favorite cousin and now Abram's wife."

As Milcah stood up, she whispered, "Do not be frightened of Ur. I will help you learn your way."

Abram carried my belongings up a ladder to a room that would be our home. I followed him up the ladder. Awkwardly, I smiled. We had never been alone, except on our wedding night. In our attic room, as we began our life together, I learned about the man whom I had married and he learned about me. At night, we lay on wool mats, holding one another and talking until we drifted to sleep. I told Abram how laughter echoed through my village's river canyon and how I dreamt of filling our home with laughing children.

I learned that Abram, too, was a dreamer. His dreams made mine seem small in comparison. Abram dreamt of opening a larger store, selling idols to traders from distant lands, and helping to spread the gods' goodwill. Abram told me that holding his father's idols made him feel strong and blessed. He described his customers—girls ripe for marriage praying for a good match, young sailors dreaming of opportunity, barren women craving children.

Each night, Abram went to our roof and knelt before an idol of the merchant god Haia. After he prayed for our family, he asked the gods to answer his customers' prayers as well. I went with him to the roof. I knelt before the *asherah* that my mother had given me and prayed for a child.

Many moons passed. One night, as we lay in our attic, Abram whispered, "I have a secret, Sarai. I have convinced my father that we should leave Ur. Haran has a market 10 times the size of ours and stands at the crossroad of all trade. Sarai, you will be the wife of a very important merchant."

I looked at Abram in disbelief. "Haran is so far away," I finally said. "How will my mother ever visit when I become pregnant and have a child?"

"The gods will see to it," Abram answered. "For now, we need to purchase camels. Our donkeys cannot carry all our belongings on the journey." From the tone of his voice and the look in his eyes, I knew not to protest.

To my great relief, Abram and Terah agreed to leave after the wheat harvest. In the year since my wedding, I had not seen my father. My father arrived with a donkey bag full of fruit from our village. As soon as I saw him, I blurted out that I would be leaving and began to cry. The next day, my father spent one third of his earnings on a map for me. I had never owned something so beautiful. The map was written on papyrus. Blue ink marked the Euphrates, Tigris, Nile, and Jordan rivers and the great seas to the south and west. A dot marked each city and town. My father pointed to Ur and Haran. He had paid a marketplace scribe to mark our village with a six-pointed star.

"Sarai, now you will always know where to find your mother and me," my father said.

Abram, Terah, and I left Ur with several servants, two camels, and Abram's nephew Lot. We followed the Euphrates in the direction that the sun sets until the river became nothing more than a wide stream surrounded by desert. Each afternoon, we waded in the refreshing waters of the Euphrates and I remembered my village. In one moon's time, we arrived at the great city of Haran. Terah rented a store in the market. We made our home in a small room behind the store. I spent my days cooking, sweeping the workshop, and taking hot idols out of the kiln. There was little time for daydreaming.

Terah was a fine craftsman, better than most sculptors in Haran. Word of his idols spread quickly, and they gained the reputation of bringing good luck. As I worked, I listened to Abram sell idols. He spoke with conviction and passion about the idols' powers. On my 16th birthday, Abram gave me a large fertility *asherah*, which Terah had crafted especially for me.

"Perhaps this year we will have a child," Abram said.

After the first rainy season ended, Terah and Abram decided that we would settle permanently in Haran. We would sell our camels and use the money to purchase a proper home.

One morning, Terah and I led the animals to a market on the outskirts of the city. I tended to the camels while Terah bargained with potential customers. He agreed on a purchase price with an Egyptian trader. When the Egyptian opened his wool bag to count out coins, a scorpion ran from the bag and bit Terah in the leg. I screamed and the other merchants quickly surrounded us. Terah doubled over in pain, holding the bite mark that almost immediately turned blotchy red. One of the merchants lifted Terah onto his camel and gal-

loped back to the city to find a medicine man. The Egyptian trader and I followed on the camels that Terah had just sold to him. The Egyptian spoke frantically, alternating between apologizing, begging my forgiveness, and praying. For
two days, Terah lingered. Abram prayed day and night to the gods, kneeling before
an idol for good health. His prayers did not help. On the third day, Terah died.

I mourned Terah like my own father and begged Abram to return to Ur.
Abram, although sorrowful at first, acted strangely free. He neglected his work
and took long walks through the desert. On those days, I worked in the store
and sold idols in his place. I told myself that Abram needed time to mourn his
father's death. Customers heard of Terah's death and rushed to purchase the last
of his idols. Soon we had very few idols left, and I began to worry.

One evening when Abram returned from the desert, his eyes danced
wildly. I distrusted his expression. Abram held my hand. He said that God had
spoken to him and given us a charge.

Abram repeated God's command: "Go forth from your native land and
from your father's house to the land that I will show you. I will make of you a
great nation, and I will bless you; I will make your name great."

I heard the words and struggled to make sense of their meaning. Stunned,
I asked, "Which god?"

"Sarai, it is not which god. The God spoke to me," Abram answered.

Almost overnight, Abram decided that idols were powerless clay and stone.
He told me, "One true God exists. We do not see God, but God is everywhere.
God created everything on earth and in the heavens. God has chosen you and me
to become a holy people. We will follow God's command and leave Haran."

I half-thought Abram was crazy. I half-thought Abram was kidding. I
knew deep down to my bones that I did not want to move even farther from
my childhood home.

Abram came to work each day, but he no longer tried to sell idols. He
preached to the customers about the one and true God. Words came out of
Abram's mouth and captured the customers' imagination. We sold very few idols,
but many customers became followers of God. They made donations simply to
be in Abram's presence. Our wealth grew. On our final night in Haran, Abram
smashed the last of his father's idols. As I swept up the clay, I mourned losing
Terah's handiwork. Without these idols, we had nothing of Terah left. Holding a
shard of clay, though, I realized I no longer believed that the idols had power.

Less than a year after God first spoke to Abram, we left Haran. Dozens of Abram's followers packed their donkey and camel bags to come with us. The poorest of the followers pledged to become our servants. With each step we took toward the Promised Land, Abram's fervor and enthusiasm grew. While he saw his dream coming closer and closer, I saw my dreams slipping away. I looked at my map to remember my home by the Euphrates. Each evening, I stared at the stars and begged God for a child.

With all his dreams, Abram could not pack a camel bag, shear a sheep, or draw water from a well, no matter how obvious the need. Soon, our camp fell into disarray. I heard my mother's voice telling me to support my husband.

In my mind, I spoke back to my mother: "Forgive me for being so bold, but I need to take charge."

Without telling Abram, I began instructing the servants, setting down rules for them to follow. I did not think that Abram noticed, until one day he heard me ordering a servant boy to be more attentive to the lambs. After the boy left, Abram whispered "thank you" into my ear.

Abram and I developed a partnership. Abram preached God's message to our servants and followers. He inspired them with his words. I made sure that these same religious seekers tended the flocks, watered the camels, cooked our meals, and cleaned up after themselves.

I became the supervisor, disciplinarian, and, most importantly, the navigator of our camp. Abram and I walked from one corner of the Middle East to another corner, only to set out walking for a third. My map guided us through our travels. Abram would say, "God tells us to go to the city of Hebron," and I would get us there. Abram would say, "God commands that we continue to the Negev desert," and I would take out the map. Soon, I had to look at the map simply to remember where I was standing, where I was going, and where I had been. Years passed and I could see myself in the map. The wrinkles on my face began to match the routes marked on the papyrus.

When I remained childless into my old age, I feared not having an heir to our legacy. I had long before given up the dream of a home filled with laughing children. I prayed for just one son, but God did not answer my prayers. I decided to give Hagar, my most trusted handmaid, to Abram. I wanted her to have a child in my place. I believed that Hagar was discreet and loyal, but I soon learned that I had judged her incorrectly. As soon as she became pregnant,

Hagar grew haughty and disobedient. She gossiped about me, mocked Abram, and neglected her work. I noticed perfumes and lotions missing from my tent. Then I smelled my favorite fragrance on Hagar. I entered my tent one day to find Hagar rummaging through my belongings. I realized that I had entrusted a thief with my most personal matters.

When Hagar gave birth to Ishmael, I could not accept him as my own. He represented my failure and my gullibility. Hagar's child would not be my legacy. I looked at Hagar playing with Ishmael and asked why couldn't it have been me? How could God reward this lying slave girl, who showed no loyalty? Bitterness filled up the spaces abandoned by my lost dreams. I took a young slave named Keturah as my handmaid and had nothing to do with Hagar or her son.

In my darkest hours, I wondered if God appreciated or even noticed me. I sacrificed my dreams to reach the Promised Land and still God had sent me no sign of my worth. At a moment of deep despair, God reached out to me. One evening, Abram returned from one of his desert walks and told me that God had changed both our names as a sign of our devotion. Abram became Abraham, and I became Sarah.

"Sarah means 'princess,'" he told me. "You know that you are God's princess—and mine, too."

At first, I did not want to give up the name Sarai. My parents had named me. My name was one last connection to them. But when people began calling me Sarah, I finally felt fully included in God's plan.

Not long afterwards, three unexpected guests passed by our camp in the heat of the afternoon. Just as he had done so many times before, Abraham asked me to cook for the guests after he had already invited them to dine with us. Once I had baked the bread, and the servant boy had boiled the meat, I sat down by the entrance to our tent for a moment's rest. I reached for my map, for we would be traveling to the Negev and I needed to plan our journey. I realized suddenly that I did not know which side of the map was up and which side was down. West blended with East and South with North. At that moment, it all seemed so ridiculous—our wanderings to follow God, Abraham's disorganization, and my attempts to create order in a mismatched camp of religious seekers, dimwitted servants, and lame camels. I started to laugh. I giggled like a young girl and roared like an old woman.

Then I heard Abraham's voice rise with excitement from under a nearby tree where he was entertaining our guests. I stopped laughing when I heard the guests saying that I was going to have a son! I laughed again, first with disbelief, then with joy. Finally, I laughed at the humor of rekindled romance between arthritic old Abraham and withered old me.

As the visitors predicted, my belly grew large and round. I thought about my mother whenever the baby kicked. So many years before, she had promised to visit when I first gave birth. I knew that my mother must have died long ago, but I hoped beyond reason that she would visit to see my child. At the first pangs of labor, I imagined the river by the village of my birth and the children jumping like lizards from rock to rock. With each contraction, I pictured another stop on our journey to God's Promised Land. When the contractions grew the most painful, I saw only my mother's face. I imagined my mother wiping sweat from my brow, even though it was just Keturah standing at my side. When my son finally emerged from my body, I called out to my mother. I knew that, in spirit, she had come to meet her grandson. I imagined my mother's laughter joining with my newborn child's cries. I named my son Isaac, after laughter. The dreams of my youth had finally come true. Why not laugh?

Sarah takes her map and places it in Lilith's ark for safekeeping. Hagar finds the ark while rifling through Sarah's tent for oils, perfumes, and lotions.

When Sarah confronts her, Hagar responds, "Now that I know about the ark, I want to add my own gift. Is my story less important than yours simply because I am a slave?"

3 | HAGAR: THE BLANKET

A HINT FROM TORAH:

Come, lift up the boy and hold him by the hand.

GENESIS 21:18

The Torah tells us very little about Hagar's background, except that she comes from Egypt and serves as Sarah's maidservant. Appropriately, her name means "stranger." The first rabbis wondered about Hagar and created an elaborate background for her. They imagined Hagar as an Egyptian princess. In one *midrash*, because Sarah's beauty captures Pharaoh's attention when she and Abraham journey to Egypt, Pharaoh gives his daughter Hagar to her as a slave. In the Torah, Sarah gives Hagar to Abraham to have a child in her place. Hagar gives birth to Ishmael, to whom Muslims trace their roots.

Let us meet Hagar…

T he other servant girls whispered and laughed like bees swarming around a hive. A low chattering buzz rose up from wherever they did their chores. I did not care that they never invited me to join in their gossip. I listened only when I overheard my name. They would whisper the words "Pharaoh" and "unloved" and "slave princess" and giggle. Sometimes, I would sneak up behind the girl talking. She would go silent and her face would turn crimson. I would laugh to myself. These girls meant nothing to me. Let them believe that I was the least favored daughter of Pharaoh, given to Sarah as a slave. I did not bother to tell them the truth about my family.

When my father was little older than a child, he began working in the limestone quarries of Egypt's Muqattam hills alongside my grandfather and uncles. My grandfather gave him a copper saw and a chisel on his 11th birthday and brought him to meet the chief quarryman. From that day until the day I was born, my father cut limestone. I am told that my father had been a proud man, with skin ruddy red from the desert sun and arms strong enough to lift limestone blocks clear over his head.

On the day of my birth, my father left my mother in the care of a midwife and went to the quarries. A birthing room is no place for a man. After three daughters, he prayed for a son. Deep in thought, my father chiseled carelessly at the limestone. Shards of stone flew into his face, blinding his right eye completely and leaving his left eye unable to see much more than shadows. The chief quarryman said that a blind man could not cut limestone. My father and mother treated me like bad luck.

After the accident, my father hunched over and shuffled as he walked. The right side of his face retracted like a spoiled melon. He was reduced to collecting dung in the alleys of Mennof-Ra, our city. He stored the dung on our roof and sold it in the market as fuel. The smell of the dung invaded our house, especially in the sweltering summer. Its stench mixed with the odors of our sweat and the fish that we caught in the Nile. Even at night, our house felt like hot grime. I shared a straw mat covered with a course wool blanket with my next elder sister. My sister and I wrestled for space as we slept and woke up in the morning sore and tired.

Like all Egyptians, we lived by the cycles of the Nile River. Each year, the Nile overflowed its banks for three moons and nourished the fields around it with black silt. The Nile's yearly gift of rich soil made vegetables and fruits plentiful, even for poor families like ours. The rhythm of childbirth in our house seemed to follow the beat of the Nile. Every other time that the Nile River overflowed, my mother gave birth. I had five younger brothers and three elder sisters, not including the two babies who died within their first moon. I figured my age to be 13.

My mother treated me as a nuisance in our smelly, crowded house. She favored my older sisters and preferred having them help her with our baby brothers. She sent me to wander the alleys and market of Mennof-Ra to look for odd jobs. She expected me to bring back my meager earnings. She told me that a few copper *sinuis* were worth more than my presence in her house. On lucky days, a rich woman would hire me to wash her laundry or a potter would send me to the Nile to draw water for his wheel. If I earned a few *sinius*, my mother smiled as she grabbed the coins. Every so often, I hid a *siniu* or two in a broken terra-cotta pot on our roof. I was saving to buy a straw mat and blanket of my own. I knew other stray boys and girls by face, not by name. They stuck together in clusters of three or four and stole fruit, clay jewelry, and make-up from the market's vendors. I avoided them.

On the days that I did not find work, I watched fishermen unload their catch from papyrus reed boats on the Nile, chuckled at old women buying perfumed wigs in the market, and listened to alley musicians play harps and hollow reed flutes. Sometimes, I ventured to a wealthy neighborhood and spied into courtyards where rich women bathed in ornamental pools and drank date wine. Their children ran naked, playing leapfrog and tug-of-war. The children's heads were shaved bald, except for a patch on top that was kept long and swung like a donkey's tail. To most people in Mennof-Ra, I was invisible. A waif in tattered white linen, I faded into the shadows cast by mud-brick homes and limestone monuments. I did not mind.

One slave boy at an idol workshop did notice me. He saw that I searched for work each day and knew that I was no thief. When he took out the trash, he allowed me to sift through the rejected idols, those with missing legs, broken noses, or evil grins. As I sorted through the idols, the slave boy talked about working to buy his freedom. Each day he had a new and farfetched dream. He spoke of owning his own idol workshop, or a plot of land to grow leeks, or a boat made out of acacia wood. I nodded, but shared nothing about myself. Soon the slave boy kept quiet as I worked. One morning, he kissed me as I sifted through the idols. I grimaced, but did not stop him. His lips felt like a fish and tasted like onions. Each morning, I let him kiss me in exchange for the idols that I took. He spoke of a new dream. He said that as soon as he gathered the modest bride-price, we would marry and make children together. The slave boy told me his name, but I have long forgotten it.

I sold my broken idols out of a basket in the market. My customers were mostly peasant farmers. They wanted good luck but could not afford it. On a profitable day, I bartered enough idols to earn a few copper coins. I preferred stationing myself near loud vendors because they attracted customers. They hawked their goods with urgent voices, promising only the best quality, best price, and best style to any passerby. Often, I stood by a tent full of eye make-up, glass beads, and papyrus sandals and a merchant who called each woman "beauty." He called me his "sweet little honey" and, sometimes, called me over to model necklaces for wealthy customers. Other days, I sat on the side of an alley, near a stand that sold barley beer. The servant at this stand gave me free samples when his master was not looking.

The only idol that I kept for myself was a statue of Bes, a dwarf-cat god who stuck its tongue out with a comic grin. I hid the Bes in my terra-cotta pot along with my copper coins. Sometimes, I snuck up to our roof at night to take out the Bes and pray. I asked for a bed of my own, a home that did not smell, and a family who thought that I brought good luck. I prayed that the servant boy would want only to kiss me, nothing more. When I finished praying, I stuck my tongue out at the Bes and imagined that we both laughed.

When I saw Sarah for the first time, the Nile had just retracted to its banks and my mother had given birth to another son. I figured my age to be 14. Sarah saw me selling my defective idols. She wore colorful clothing and blue eye makeup, clear marks of a visitor from the North. Egyptians wore white linen and dark eyeliner. Short and slender, Sarah carried herself like a wife of Pharaoh. She tilted her chin slightly upward and rustled her long robes as she walked. She did not smile broadly; rather she puckered her lips into a tight grin. Sarah looked like wealth. Two slave girls followed behind her and carried her purchases.

Sarah frowned when the merchant with the papyrus sandals called her "beauty." She ignored him and walked up to me. Sarah looked me up and down. I felt uneasy as she studied my arms, hips, and legs, like a customer sizing up her options. Finally, she introduced herself. She called herself "Sarai" when we first met. When Sarah started asking questions, I gave the shortest answers possible. I had no need for a nosy foreigner.

"I have noticed you selling idols over the last few days. Hard work, is it not?'" Sarah asked.

"I suppose," I answered.

"My husband's father was a fine sculptor of idols. I once tried to make an idol myself and remember the clay as cool to the hands. Did you make these idols?" she asked.

"No," I answered, and looked away.

Sarah did not seem to notice my irritation. Or maybe she chose to ignore it. She continued, "Do you like spending your day in the market? Most girls I know spend their days at home, helping their mothers."

"I am not missing anything at home. I am better off here," I said.

Sarah had not even looked at the idols. She was taking up space and crowding out potential customers.

"Do you believe in the idols that you are selling?" she asked.

"If I say 'yes,' will you buy one?'" I answered sharply.

She smiled, and made me an offer. "I need a young woman to be a handmaid. I want somebody who works hard and keeps to herself. My other young servants gossip and complain," Sarah said, looking at the slave girls whispering several feet away. "I'm trying to have a baby, you understand. I do not have the time to pamper a handmaid."

When Sarah said "handmaid," I thought to myself, "slave." I suppose that "handmaid" sounds better, but I was not fooled. As Sarah explained it, I would do the wash, cook, and care for a baby, if she was lucky enough to have one. If we got along well, I would help with her makeup and hair in the morning. Sarah told me that I would get my mat to sleep on and I would share a tent with only three other girls. I did not want to appear too eager, so I told Sarah that I would think about her offer.

I was ready to see something other than the same poor neighborhood, with the same poor people and the same poor future. If I stayed, my only prospect was to marry the slave boy and hope one of his dreams would come true. The next morning, I left with only my hidden copper coins, the Bes, and the blanket that I shared with my sister. When my family noticed that the blanket was missing, they would know I was gone. I thought about saying good-bye to the slave boy, but decided against it.

"Remember your role as a handmaid, Hagar," Sarah told me on the day that I left Mennof-Ra. "When I make a decision, you support me. You never gossip. Be discreet with the other servant girls."

Sarah and I walked to their camp just north of Mennof-Ra on the Nile. Dozens of black wool tents formed a rough circle. Donkeys, sheep, and goats roamed freely through the camp. On the outskirts of the camp, cattle and camels grazed. Sarah showed me the tent that I was to share. It was one of the smallest tents, but it smelled like fresh air. A mat was already set up for me in the corner. I placed my blanket on it. We arrived in time for the midday meal. Sarah sat me with the other slave girls to eat dark bread and cheese. I recognized the two slave girls from the market. When they smiled at me, I looked away. The other servants wore the colorful clothing of Canaan. Several had papyrus sandals from Egypt. They spoke with thick accents and drilled me with questions. I gave one- or two-word answers, and soon they ignored me.

I knew better than to become friends with the other people in camp. I kept to myself and rarely spoke to the other girls. Each morning, I helped Sarah dress and put on her makeup. She complained about everybody. She called Abraham's shepherds dimwitted and the other servant girls lazy. I held no affection for Sarah, but certainly did not want to fall out of favor with her.

We left the Nile basin for the Negev desert. Dry sand replaced the rich soil of Egypt. Without the rhythms of the Nile to guide me, I soon lost track of my age. Sarah, though, was very conscious of the passage of time. Each moon, she got the periods of women and cried. Her face began to wrinkle, and gray strands contrasted with her auburn hair. No baby came her way. I tried to act sympathetic, but in my mind I would think, "She is too old for a baby. Does she not understand?"

Sarah told me about her faith in her god. "Hagar, God will see that I have a child," she said. "Do you believe that God gets us through the hard times?"

I nodded my head, but said nothing. I had more faith in myself than in a god. Except for the Bes, I had never prayed. Most people in camp talked like Sarah, trusting in an unseen god for their fortune and protection. They said that this god had spoken to Abraham and promised him land and many descendants. I wondered why he continued to believe, since he and Sarah were spending their years wandering the desert with no children of their own. I kept my doubts to myself.

At first, Abraham ignored me. I assumed that he did not know my name. But then, late one afternoon, he approached me while I washing Sarah's clothing. The expression in Abraham's eyes reminded me of the slave boy when he kissed me.

"Sarah says you come from a large family with many children," Abraham said.

"I had three older sisters and six younger brothers when I left," I answered, turning my back to return to the laundry.

"You must know how to swaddle a baby and rock him to sleep," he said, attempting conversation again.

"My mother and older sisters mostly cared for the babies," I answered. I tried not to look at him.

"You must dream of holding your first child," he said. I heard hope in his voice.

Abraham's prying made my stomach turn in knots. I did not answer, pretending to be too busy to talk. I breathed deeply when Abraham walked away. He did not give up. A couple of days later, I was bent over cleaning Sarah's tent. Abraham came up behind me and touched my back. Startled, I jumped. He began asking more questions: "Do you like being a handmaid? It must be hard for an independent girl like you."

"You and Sarah treat me well," I answered, catching my breath. "But I am used to having freedom. Do you not like your freedom? Would you want to give it up?'"

I knew that I had said too much. I quickly turned away and went back to cleaning.

"We are all servants of God," he said apologetically as he left.

Several days later, Sarah approached me. She looked tense.

"Please come to my tent this evening after your chores," she said sternly. "Abraham and I wish to talk with you."

Had the other servant girls spread lies about me? While I baked the evening's bread, I came to the conclusion that Sarah and Abraham were planning to throw me out of camp. I panicked. It would take me at least three moons to walk back to Egypt, if I could even find my way. Besides, my family certainly had forgotten about me long ago.

As soon as I arrived at the tent, Sarah began, "Hagar, you know that Abraham and I have been trying to have a baby for a long time."

I nodded. Abraham had his eyes to the ground.

"I have come to think of you as a daughter," Sarah continued.

I thought to myself, "I hope that they do not want to adopt me."

"Abraham and I are getting older," Sarah continued. "I have come to realize that I probably will not get pregnant. Not at my age. My periods of women have begun to wane."

"Yes," I whispered.

"Abraham and I still want a child very badly. It has always been my dream to raise a son or daughter," Sarah said with a little more force. "Hagar, would you consider having a child with Abraham for me?"

"What?" I answered, looking back and forth between Sarah and Abraham.

Her question shocked me, but I saw longing in both their eyes. I knew that they were serious.

"You and Abraham would have a child and give the baby to me to raise," Sarah explained. "Of course, you could help care for the baby, if you wanted."

I looked squarely at Sarah, then at Abraham. I thought about what to do next. In the middle of the desert, a slave, no family and friends, I had to rely on myself. I thought back to the vendors hawking their goods in the market.

I answered, "What will you give me in exchange?"

Abraham looked up and spoke for the first time.

"Hagar, as soon as the baby is born, you will get your freedom," he answered quietly. "You will always have a home among us, but as a free woman. You will get your own tent and some items of wealth. I will pay you a generous bride-price for a girl of your status."

I thought about Abraham touching me and felt ill. I thought about having my own tent and felt nervous with excitement. I thought about having a child and felt relieved that I would be able to give that child to Sarah. I thought about the alternative. If I turned Abraham and Sarah down, they might very well treat me as the lowliest slave in the camp or, worse, abandon me. I realized that I had little choice. So, I agreed.

Each night, Abraham's servant Eliezer came to my tent when Abraham was ready. He escorted me to Abraham's tent, but I went into the tent alone. Thankfully, Abraham did not speak and moved quickly. His hands were cold, and his eyes asked me to forgive him. Two moons later, I was pregnant.

With a baby in my belly, I would soon have wealth. I pictured the rich women of Mennof-Ra drinking wine and imagined myself among them. I thought of Sarah's fine makeup and clothing and imagined myself wearing them. I snuck into Sarah's tent to borrow fine lotions to rub onto my belly. I wanted to protect my child, for this baby had become my greatest asset. I felt that I had a sapphire or emerald growing within me. My child would be a gem for both Sarah and me. I began to slow down at my work, for I did not want to strain my body with this baby inside.

One evening, the other slave girls were cooking dinner. I walked up for a taste.

"Does your round belly permit you to stop working?" one girl asked. "Can a pregnant slave girl no longer cook?"

I spoke without caution. "I am carrying a precious child for Sarah, since she is barren," I said. "Is that not labor enough? Abraham's hands felt like cold leather and his joints cracked when he touched me. I have done my duty."

Just then, I realized that Sarah was standing behind me. The other slaves took one step back from the fire pit and then another. I heard giggling as they disappeared.

"I will not have dishonor in my camp," said Sarah. "We chose you precisely because I trusted that you would not talk about our arrangement. Now I am going make you work so hard that you will not have time to talk or steal from me like a common thief."

From that day on, Sarah gave me the most difficult jobs in camp—cleaning up after the sheep, folding the tents, and carrying the water. She did not care that I was pregnant with her husband's child. I collapsed each night in my tent.

With too much work, a child in my belly, and not a friend in the world, I decided to run away. I would make my way back to Egypt. Perhaps the slave boy would remember me after all these years. We could marry. I started out into the desert without saying good-bye. For two days, I walked through the wilderness. Sand flew into my face, and I drank all my water. My determination wore off, and thirst took over. Lost and covered with dust and sweat, I collapsed by a cool water spring. As I drank, I realized that I would not make it to Egypt alive. I closed my eyes to rest and think.

A voice spoke to me: "Hagar, go back to Sarah and submit to her harsh treatment."

I thought to myself, "Who is this voice? Why would I want to submit myself to Sarah again? What could I possibly gain?"

"I will make your offspring too numerous to count. You will bear a child and name him Ishmael," declared the voice.

The promise sounded familiar, like the charge that Abraham said his god had given him. Perhaps I was hallucinating. The only god to whom I had ever spoken was the Bes, who had never responded. Nonetheless, I took the advice. Where else was I going to go? I went back to camp and suffered through Sarah's harsh treatment. A few moons later, I gave birth to a son. I was stunned when Abraham, indeed, named him Ishmael. I brought Ishmael to Sarah. Sarah did not even look at him.

"I do not want your son," she said, and walked away.

Abraham and Sarah kept their promise and gave me my freedom, a tent, and a few bracelets of copper. Otherwise, I was left to raise my son on my own. I pitched our tent on the outskirts of camp, and everybody left us alone. Only Abraham would visit. Late at night, he would arrive and insist that I wake up Ishmael. Abraham would hold Ishmael and tell him stories of his god.

One new moon, shocking news spread throughout our camp. Sarah was pregnant. As she grew larger, she waddled around camp and expected everybody else to tend to her like a princess. I kept my distance. Abraham visited Ishmael less often. Many nights, the poor boy waited up to see a father who never came. When we no longer heard any sounds in camp, Ishmael would fall asleep in disappointment.

When Isaac was three years old, Abraham planned a great feast to celebrate his weaning. Ishmael heard the sounds of the party and pleaded to go. I held his hand, and together we walked to the edge of the festivities. Ishmael saw Abraham holding a ball and playing with Isaac. He broke free of my grip and ran to join his father.

"Play with me, Father," called Ishmael, smiling and grabbing at the ball.

Sarah looked at Ishmael and frowned. Abraham gave the ball to Ishmael, patted him on the head, and walked away, carrying Isaac. Ishmael held the ball in his hands and began to wail. The next morning, Abraham came to my tent. He ordered Ishmael and me to leave camp.

"Hagar, you know that I care about Ishmael, but you both must leave. It is just better this way," he said.

"Better for whom?" I asked, but Abraham did not answer. "I've made it on my own all these years. I can make it without you."

I put my meager possessions into a knapsack. Abraham gave us food and water. Ishmael and I walked into the heat of the wilderness.

I said to myself, "I don't need Abraham, I don't need Sarah, I don't need anybody."

But soon the heat grew stronger. Ishmael and I drank our supply of water. I worried about lions, snakes, and scorpions. By early afternoon of the second day, with no well, spring, or river in sight, the hallucinations began. Ishmael started to lag behind me. He cried. As the sun moved across the sky, I was certain that he would die.

I found a bush and put him underneath it. Then I walked away. I could not watch him. He called out for me, but I ignored his cries. I sat down, and once again I was on my own.

Then I heard a voice from the heavens saying, "Go hold your son."

I stood up, and the voice said, "Reach out to your son."

I walked to Ishmael and heard, "You are not alone. You have Ishmael."

I put my arms around Ishmael and was told, "Care for Ishmael, and he will care for you."

I took the coarse wool blanket from my knapsack and piled it as a pillow on my lap. I put Ishmael's head on the blanket and looked up. Right in front of me, a well of water appeared. I gave Ishmael water to drink. I hugged him and then drank myself. For the first time in my life, I was not alone. I realized that God had spoken to me. I had Ishmael. I needed my son, and he needed me. Together, we would survive.

On the day that Abraham throws Hagar out of camp, she sneaks into Sarah's tent and takes Lilith's ark. Hagar places her blanket in the ark.

After one moon's time, Abraham comes looking for Hagar in her desert oasis.

"Did you take something that belongs to my wife?" he asks Hagar.

"It belongs to me also," Hagar says weakly, handing Lilith's ark to Abraham.

Abraham returns the ark to Sarah's tent, where Rebekah eventually finds it.

4 | REBEKAH: THE WATER JUG

A HINT FROM TORAH:

They called Rebekah and said to her,
"Will you go with this man?"
And she said, "I will."   GENESIS 24:58

Rebekah, the second matriarch, is Abraham's grandniece. She
marries Isaac, and together they have Jacob and Esau. Her name
means "tied" or "bound." Like Sarah and Abraham, she grows
up among idolaters yet feels bound to live a life with a different
purpose. Rebekah enters the biblical story at a time of conflict
and transition: Not long before we meet Rebekah, Abraham
receives a command from God to bind and sacrifice Isaac. An
angel stops Abraham in the moment before he kills his son. This
test of faith is known as the *Akedah*. Sarah dies at the beginning
of the next chapter of Genesis. A well-known and commonly
accepted *midrash* attributes Sarah's death to the shock and grief of
hearing about the Akedah. After Sarah's death, Abraham decides it
is time to find a wife for Isaac. Not wanting Isaac to marry a
Canaanite woman, Abraham sends his servant Eliezer back to his
homeland to find a bride for his son. Eliezer journeys to the
town of Nahor, near Haran. When Eliezer encounters Rebekah
by a well, God sends a sign that she is destined to be Isaac's wife.
Rebekah chooses to leave her home and go to Canaan to marry
Isaac, whom she does not know.

Let us meet Rebekah...

The feeblest lamb, the runt of herd, caught himself again in a bramble bush. I saw just a glimpse of his brown speckled fleece, but the whole valley could hear him bleat. His cries echoed off the mountains. For the third time since morning, I went to free him. As I lifted his body, dusty lanolin from his fleece rubbed off on my face and thistles scratched my legs. I did not mind rescuing this lamb. He was scrawny and his fleece would never make fine wool, but he was curious and smart. The lamb squirmed under my arm as I carried him back to his mother. I released him onto the ground, and he poked underneath his mother's belly to nurse. The ewe steadied herself. She looked up at me with eyes that shone like river rocks and seemed to say, "You treat him too well." She favored the runt's larger and stronger twin.

The runt's mother was my first ewe, a gift from my parents for my 10th birthday. As a lamb, she had chased after me like a younger sister, nuzzling her head into my leg and drinking water from my cupped hands. When my older brother Laban drove our family's herd out to pasture, I would trail behind him with my one little lamb. By watching Laban, I learned how to recognize the best grazing lands—those with shade trees and without too many thistles. This spring and last, my ewe had given birth to lambs. She was a mother, and I had not yet become a woman. At least my father, Bethuel, now trusted me with the family's herd.

Each morning, I guided half our herd to the village well. There, I met my friend Adinah and we joined our herds together. Laban shepherded the other half of our family's herd with his friends. The most difficult part of the day was moving the sheep out to pasture. I drove the sheep from behind, while Adinah stayed on the herd's perimeters to keep the sheep together. Once the sheep were safely grazing, we could rest under an olive tree and drink from our water skins. We talked about which boys in our village would make the best husbands and which boys were the most pleasing to the eyes. We laughed a little louder when Laban and his friends grazed their herds near us. Adinah thought Laban was handsome.

"Adinah," I said. "My brother is like the ancient shepherd king Dumuzi. He envisions himself marrying a goddess and becoming a god himself. He already acts like a god in our house."

Adinah lived farther from the valley's grazing pastures and left for home when the sun began its descent. I could keep my sheep in the pasture until the sun nearly hit the horizon and the sky turned pink and orange. I never told Adinah, of course, but I often enjoyed the solitude after she left. My grandfather and I had hiked through our valley many times when I was a young girl. He showed me places where the hawks nested and entrances to underground caves. He taught me to use the jelly of aloe plants on bug bites and how to recognize the tracks of jackals and foxes. I missed my grandfather. He had died during the most recent sheep-shearing season. My grandmother Milcah said that, by remembering my grandfather, I could keep his spirit alive. I felt my grandfather's spirit in our valley, where he had come to find his brother Abram's spirit.

Around our fire pit, my grandfather had often talked about Uncle Abram and Aunt Sarai. He repeated their story so many times that it became my story as well. My grandfather and Abram were born in the faraway city of Ur. In search of wealth and good fortune, Abram, Terah, and Sarai left Ur and went to Haran, along with a nephew named Lot. Nobody ever talked about Lot, except to say he was trouble. My grandparents stayed behind in Ur. My grandmother had just given birth to her third son, my uncle Kemuel, and could not leave. My grandfather promised my grandmother that one day they would join the family in Haran.

Eventually, my grandfather kept his promise. My grandparents outgrew their home in Ur when my grandmother bore her eighth son, my father. My grandparents packed their belongings on camels, placed their youngest sons on donkeys, and brought along servants to herd their sheep. Slowly, they journeyed to Haran. When my grandparents arrived at the gates of Haran, the city's elders told them tragic news: Namtar, a demon of death, had visited our family. Terah was dead. My grandparents tore their clothing and covered themselves with ashes. The city elders and the townsfolk alike came to comfort them.

Each visitor told the same strange tale. After Terah's death, they said, Abram had changed. Peasants saw Abram often in the valley, staring at the heavens and talking to himself. They feared he had lost his mind. Abram claimed that an eternal and all-powerful god had spoken to him. One new moon, Abram and Sarai had left Haran with Lot and many new converts. Nobody in Haran or our valley had heard from them since.

When my grandfather rose from mourning his father, he hiked through our valley for the first time. My grandfather joked that, although God did not speak to him, the lush grazing land told him to settle. My grandparents built a large house in our valley. When my grandfather brought sheep to market in Haran, he proudly told other shepherds about our valley's rich pastures. Soon, a small shepherd village emerged. My grandmother convinced my grandfather to name the village "Nahor" after himself.

"If Sarai and Abram come searching for us, the name will guide them," she reasoned.

As I herded sheep, I often wondered where in our valley God had spoken to Abram. I once asked Laban about Abram, and he just laughed.

"You do not believe that a god actually spoke to Abram, do you?" he mocked. "Abram lost his mind in this valley. If you think about Abram too much, you will lose your mind as well."

One autumn day, fate brought me to where God had spoken to Abram. Once again, that scrawny runt of a lamb had wandered off. While he was climbing up a rocky crag, his hoof had become trapped in a crevice between two boulders. I ran to rescue him and found myself on a small cliff that I had not seen before.

I heard a soft voice say, "*Lechi lach*, go forth. Leave your parents' home and go to the land that I will show you."

I had no doubts about who was speaking. God's voice sounded like a soft and comforting lullaby. I knew that my life would never be the same. I eagerly waited for God to speak to me again.

Just a few days later, when I was drawing water from the village well at day's end, I heard God's voice. God's words felt like my grandmother's hug and sounded like running water.

God commanded, "*Lechi lach*, Rebekah, my child. I will make your name great. Your descendants will number in the thousands. Your journey will start at this well."

As I continued drawing water, the jug felt lighter or my arms seemed stronger or maybe it was a little of both. After that day, I began to talk to people about how I had heard from God, how God had called to me. I wanted to tell the world about God's peaceful voice and the serenity that I felt. I talked about my calling a lot, perhaps too much. Soon I noticed that our neighbors were looking at me in disbelief.

I heard them whisper to one another, "This girl, she thinks that the gods spoke to her!"

I came home one night and my brother Laban grumbled, "Who do you think you are? The gods are talking to you? Everybody thinks that you have lost your mind. Be quiet already about this 'calling' of yours."

As I helped my grandmother spin yarn, she spoke more forcefully than I had ever heard her speak before.

"How can you believe that Abram's god called on you?" said my grandmother. "Your grandfather, my Nahor, spent his years in our valley searching for answers about Abram. He died still wondering. This god took Abram away from my Nahor and Sarai away from me. Rebekah, it is time that we forget Abram's god."

My nursemaid, Deborah, who had helped raise me since birth, pulled me aside and said, "Rebekah, I know you are a good girl. Maybe you did hear from your god. If you did, I am happy for you. Still, talking about it so often makes everybody nervous."

At least Deborah believed that maybe God had spoken to me.

I woke up one night to my parents' voices deep in conversation in the next room. "I think there is something wrong with her," said my father. "Who has ever heard such a story? A god talking to a girl. Soon, she will be ready to marry. No boy will want a bride who is soft in the mind."

My mother calmed my father down. "When I was her age, I dreamt that I had a great-grandson named Joseph who became an Egyptian noble. Many girls have visions of grandeur. Bethuel, it will pass."

Whenever somebody doubted me, I thought of God's serene voice. I heard my future in that voice. The course of my life seemed so clear in front of me. A sense of calm came over my body and excitement beat in my heart. The two corners of my lips pulled up into a smile. I told myself to trust my instincts and listen to that small, but persistently loud, voice in my head. After God spoke to me, I spent a lot of time by the well. I would silently repeat God's words, "Your journey will start at this well." Many moons passed, and I heard nothing from God. I began to doubt whether God had ever spoken to me. Deborah wiped away my tears and gave me a small clay idol.

"Look at this idol and remember your god. You can still believe, even if your god does not speak to you," said Deborah.

Not to offend Deborah, I took the idol, even though I did not believe that it had any power.

One evening, Laban and I stood by the well, drawing water for the sheep. I heard a buzz. At first, I thought a bee had flown into my ear. Then I recognized the voice. It was soft but steady. It refreshed me like a cool swim in summer and sounded like the wind.

God whispered, "Rebekah, my child, the moment of your calling has almost arrived. Be yourself and you will know what to do. Lechi lach, go forth."

Calmly and confidently, I turned to Laban and said, "I have just heard the voice of God. God remembered me and my calling."

Laban just started to laugh. "You and your 'calling.' Do you not know that the gods talk only to important people? Not to stupid shepherd girls."

"God can speak to each of us. You just need to listen," I retorted.

I turned my back to Laban and began to draw water again. This time when I picked up my clay jug, it felt as light as the finest fleece.

The next day, I avoided Laban. I took my sheep out to pasture with Adinah, but made an excuse to leave early. Just after the sun reached its peak, I herded my sheep back to the village well. I sat down a distance away under an olive tree and tried to make sense of it all. What did God want with me? The women of the village came and went, drawing water for their flocks and families. I barely acknowledged them.

By early evening, the women had returned to their homes and I was alone. I looked up and saw a dusty, sweat-soaked traveler walking toward the well. Ten servants and 10 camels, laden with bags, followed him. Curiously, I knew the stranger's name—Eliezer. He was Uncle Abram's most trusted servant. I hurried to the well and drew water into my jug.

Before I could offer water to him, Eliezer asked, "Please, let me sip a little water from your jug."

I heard raw hope in his voice. I quickly gave him my jug and told him to drink. Not thinking of the labor required, I said to him, "I will also draw water for your camels."

The clay jug felt like silver in my hands. Drawing water was effortless. Eliezer gazed at me silently as I worked. After I finished filling the troughs for the camels, Eliezer placed two gold bracelets on my arms and gave me a golden nose ring. I did not question such a generous gift from a mere stranger, a gift that could even signify a betrothal. I understood that it was part of my calling. Eliezer asked my name and whether he and the other men could stay with my family for the night. I sensed that he already knew the answer.

"I am Rebekah, the daughter of Bethuel, the son of Milcah and Nahor," I replied. "There is plenty of feed for the camels at our home and also room for you and your men to spend the night."

Eliezer bowed low in front of me and said, "Blessed is the God of Sarah and Abraham. God has guided me to the home of their family."

For a moment, I felt confused. "You do mean the God of Abram and Sarai, do you not?" I asked with a quiver in my voice.

Eliezer answered, "God changed their names, Rebekah. Abram and Sarai are now called Abraham and Sarah. Rest assured, I do speak of your family and your God."

When I heard the word "family," I remembered my parents and grandmother. I led Eliezer back to our house and went inside to announce his arrival. As soon as Laban saw the bracelets and nose ring, he hurried to meet Eliezer.

"Why are you still standing outside?" he asked Eliezer and the other men. "I will personally make sure that our house is ready for you. Come, I will get servants to feed your camels and bring water to bathe your feet."

Our home flew into a whirlwind, like a dust storm in the desert. Laban and my father talked eagerly with Eliezer and his men. Deborah organized sleeping quarters for our guests. My mother and I helped our servants prepare a feast. My grandmother sat in disbelief.

She kept repeating, "Nahor, after all these years, Sarai and Abram sent word back to us."

"Grandmother, they are called Abraham and Sarah now," I called to her, but she did not hear me.

Before we ate, Eliezer insisted on sharing his story and the purpose of his visit. We did not protest, for Eliezer's words interested us far more than even fine food.

Eliezer began, "I am Abraham's senior servant. God has blessed my master Abraham and Sarah with many servants and much wealth and livestock. When Sarah and Abraham were already old, God blessed them and Sarah gave birth to a son, whom she named Isaac. Abraham made me pledge to journey back to you, his family, to find a wife for Isaac. An angel of God has guided me to Rebekah."

My family looked at me. I smiled awkwardly and turned my eyes to the ground.

Eliezer continued, "When I arrived at your village well this evening, I asked God to send a sign and identify the maiden destined to become Isaac's wife. I said to God, 'Let me ask a young woman for a drink. If she gives me her water jug and also offers to water my camels, then I will know she is Isaac's intended wife.' I had scarcely finished praying when your Rebekah came to draw water. When I asked her for a drink, she gave her water jug to me and volunteered to draw water for the camels."

My father and brother stood silently, perhaps weighing whether Eliezer spoke the truth.

Eliezer continued with a sense of urgency. "Please let me know. Have I been successful in my quest?'"

I knew Eliezer spoke of my calling. Silently, I pleaded with my father and brother: "Answer yes." Laban stared at the riches that Eliezer had unpacked onto a colorful rug near the front door. My father looked at me, then followed Laban's gaze.

Laban, nodding at our father, said, "The matter was decreed by God."

My father declared, "Let Rebekah be a wife to your master's son."

I sighed with relief, although my stomach knotted in apprehension. My grandmother began to cry. My mother hugged me, and I felt her tears on my neck. Eliezer gave us gifts of gold, silver, and fine garments. I scarcely looked at the gifts, but Laban sat in the middle of gold and silver, gloating over his good fortune.

We sat down to eat, but I remember very little about the feast. My mind raced between thoughts of God's calling, my engagement to a stranger, and the sadness of leaving my home. After our meal, Deborah showed Eliezer and his men to their sleeping quarters. When our guests were safely out of earshot, my family began to talk.

"I have only imagined such wealth," began Laban, holding two silver bowls. "Do you think that Eliezer will give us more gifts before he leaves?'"

My father looked at the gifts and said, "Rebekah, you will live in luxury. I never dreamt of such a good marriage for you. Maybe Abraham's god is truly the most powerful."

"First, I lost Sarai. And now you, Rebekah?" cried my grandmother. "Why was my family chosen by this god?"

My mother sat silently. Then she spoke deliberately. "Bethuel, you have exchanged Rebekah's hand in marriage for riches. I need time to say good-bye to my child. Eliezer must not take her too soon."

The next morning, I awoke early. I rushed to Adinah's home to tell her all that had happened. Adinah saw the nose ring and bracelets and squealed in delight.

"My calling has begun," I told her. I spoke excitedly about Eliezer, his caravan of riches, and my engagement to Isaac. Adinah told me to slow down. She wanted to hear every detail. When I finished my story, Adinah looked lonely, as if I had already left. She tried to smile.

"I am jealous," she said with a tiny laugh. "You will marry an exotic foreigner."

Adinah and I linked our arms and walked back to my family's home. When we arrived, we heard loud voices inside. My parents and Laban were arguing with Eliezer. Adinah and I stood next to the doorway and listened.

Eliezer said, "Let me take Rebekah today and return to my master."

My mother trembled as she spoke. "Bethuel and Laban, please appeal to Eliezer on my behalf."

"Everything will work out," said my father, trying to console my mother. But his voice sounded uncertain. He and my brother whispered to one another. Then Laban spoke up.

"Let Rebekah remain with us for at least 10 days," he said. "Eliezer, think about my mother. She cannot be separated from her only daughter so quickly. Besides, do you not want to visit the famous market in Haran? Perhaps there are more gifts that you need to purchase."

Eliezer persisted. "Please do not delay my return to my master, now that God has made me successful in my quest."

My father composed himself and said, "Let us call Rebekah and ask her to decide."

Adinah and I stepped in the room. My father frowned on my eavesdropping.

He asked, "Will you leave with this man?'"

I looked at my mother and grandmother, but thought of God's voice. I hesitated with my answer for only a moment.

I declared, "I will."

My voice sounded like a lullaby and the wind. My future was ordained.

I hugged my mother and said, "I am sorry, but this is my calling. Through my memories, your spirit will stay with me."

"I know," whispered my mother.

My grandmother came forward. "Will you hug Sarai for me? Please tell her how I have missed her," she said. "I will miss you as well."

"I will send back word of my well-being," I replied. "I do not want you to worry, as you have about Sarah."

By the time the sun hit its peak in the sky, my belongings were packed on top of a camel. My parents gave me the most wonderful gift, better even than all the gold and silver that Eliezer had brought. Deborah had asked to go with me. I turned around and there were Deborah and Eliezer talking quietly to one another. He reached into a bag and put a small gold bracelet onto her arm. She grinned.

My father helped me onto a camel. My grandmother, my mother, and Adinah stepped forward. Together they blessed me: "O, dear sister! May you have numerous descendants. May your children always be safe and secure."

I smiled and said, "I will treasure your blessing always."

As Eliezer led our caravan out of our valley, I looked over my shoulder until I could no longer see my family.

I called out, "May you have peace." My voice echoed through our valley.

It took more than one moon to reach Canaan, but the time passed quickly. Often, as we traveled, the only sound was the camels' hooves against the desert sand. Surrounded by this quiet rhythm, I reflected on how quickly my life had changed. As the caravan carried me toward my future, I grew excited to meet the legendary Sarah and Abraham of my grandfather's stories. Would Sarah treat me as a daughter? Would Abraham believe in my calling? I especially wondered about Isaac. Was he handsome? Did he laugh like his name? Did God also speak to him? Would we grow to love one another?

In the evenings, around the fire pit, I asked Eliezer about Sarah, Abraham, and Isaac. Over time, I noticed how he gently avoided my questions. I began to grow suspicious. I knew that Eliezer was hiding something. On the day that we crossed the Jordan River into Canaan, Deborah pulled me aside.

She said, "Rebekah, my sweet girl, I fear that Eliezer has not shared everything about Sarah, Abraham, and Isaac with you. Eliezer has confided in me. I feel that I must tell you the truth before we meet Isaac."

I sat down to listen.

Deborah's body shook as she spoke. "Several moons ago, Abraham heard God's voice command him to sacrifice Isaac as a burnt offering. Abraham gathered his knife, some wood, and Isaac. They walked for three days in the desert. On the third day, Abraham bound Isaac to an altar. As Abraham raised his knife over Isaac, an angel stopped him at the last possible moment. But the damage was already done. When Sarah learned that Abraham had nearly killed Isaac, she went into shock and died of anger and grief. Abraham and Isaac no longer speak to one another."

When Deborah finished her story, I began to cry. I mourned my lost dream. For the first time, I feared my unknown future. I grieved for Sarah and the loss of never meeting her. I would have no mother in Canaan. I tried to envision Isaac, but no longer could imagine him without seeing a knife. I walked away in silence. Deborah called after me, but I needed solitude. I craved guidance.

I sat by myself in the desert and looked up at the numberless stars above. The desert wind blew gently, and I recognized God's voice in its sound.

God said, "Rebekah, now you understand why I chose you. Go to Isaac and comfort him. Isaac no longer wants to hear me. He is like the lamb caught in a bramble bush. He bleats in silent pain and awaits rescue. You have become my most important messenger."

The next evening, we reached the Negev desert. I saw a lone man walking toward our caravan. As he drew nearer, I saw that his muscles were firm and his face had finely chiseled features. My heart beat quickly, and I felt the faint stirrings of desire. Distracted, I nearly fell as I dismounted the camel.

"Who is that man walking toward us?" I asked Eliezer.

"That is my master Isaac," he replied.

I covered my face with a dark veil as a sign of modesty and respect. Isaac stood silently in front of me. Eliezer told Isaac how God had guided him to my village and to me. When Eliezer had finished, he left me alone with Isaac.

Isaac did not speak, so I said, "The God of your mother called upon me and brought me to you."

Isaac lifted my veil, and I saw his face more clearly. His features were beautiful, but his eyes were hollow and expressionless. I felt a chill of wind.

Then Isaac spoke. "My mother has died. You may make her tent your own."

Isaac carried my bags through camp. Servants worked at churning milk into cheese, weaving, and skinning meat. When they saw us, they stood and watched in silence. We entered one of the largest tents in the camp. Sarah's belongings were covered with a thick layer of sand and dust.

"I will send a servant girl to clean," Isaac said, turning to leave.

"Please stay," I called after him. "There will be time to clean later. Talk to me. I have wondered about you for so long."

Isaac looked at me, and I noticed the smallest spark of interest in his eyes. He picked two cushions off the ground and shook the dust off them. He motioned for me to sit. I listened to Isaac. He told me about his mother's affection and jealousy, about his half brother Ishmael whom he never saw as a rival, and about his father's young new wife, Keturah. Isaac told me nothing of Abraham nearly killing him, nor did I ask. When Isaac finished, I began my story. When I spoke of my grandmother and how she never forgot Sarah, I leaned over and held Isaac for the first time. In my arms, he found comfort. I felt his heart beat. In that moment, I understood my calling.

Rebekah takes her water jug and places it in Lilith's ark. She safeguards the ark for many years. When Rebekah meets Rachel and Leah, she gives them the ark.

"Be kind about one another when you tell your stories," she warns.

5 | RACHEL: THE IDOLS

A HINT FROM TORAH:

Now Laban had two daughters;
the name of the older one was Leah,
and the name of the younger was Rachel.
Leah had weak eyes;
Rachel was shapely and beautiful. GENESIS 29:16–17

Rachel is best known as Jacob's favorite wife and the mother of Joseph and Benjamin. Rachel's name fittingly means "ewe," since she is a shepherdess. An intense rivalry exists between Rachel and her older sister, Leah. Both sisters marry their cousin Jacob. After Jacob works seven years for Rachel's hand in marriage, he is tricked into marrying Leah instead. After his bridal week with Leah, Jacob also marries Rachel, pledging himself to another seven years of servitude. The Torah only hints at the emotional effect of this rivalry on the two sisters.

Let us meet Rachel…

My elder sister Leah's eyes were so sensitive that, when the first sliver of sun shone into our room, she would awake with a startle. She stirred in her wood-framed bed, its rawhide cords creaking as they rubbed together. Until we married, Leah and I slept a few arm's lengths away from one another on matching beds that our grandfather Bethuel had given us before he died.

He had told us with pride, "Now, my two princesses need not sleep on floor mats like peasants."

I would feign irritation when Leah tossed and turned in bed. Each morning, I snapped, "Leah, Grandfather would take back your bed if he could hear all the noise that you are making. You might even wake our brothers in the next room."

In truth, I did not resent being woken up early. First thing in the morning, I was privy to a secret, to a marvel that neither Leah nor I could explain. For just a few minutes each morning, Leah's eyes sparkled like twin emeralds in clear, deep water. Her eye lashes curled unnaturally inward, though, reminding us that soon her eyes' clarity would soon disappear. As we dressed, Leah's right eye began to wander upward, making her appear increasingly dimwitted. By the time Leah finished braiding my hair, her right eye focused straight to the sky. Her eyes began oozing tears, for her eyelashes were curled so far inward that they could not keep out sand or dust. By the end of the day, her eyes looked like two mismatched rocks caught in stale water. Boys in our village taunted Leah and claimed that the night demon Lilith had taken possession of her eyes. I grew angry when our brothers did nothing to stop their gossip.

Our mother, Adinah, climbed the ladder to our room each morning, bringing yogurt, mulberries, and bread for us to eat together. She would never admit it, but Leah and I knew that she came to check on Leah's eyes. Our mother simply said that our room brought back good memories. We slept in a room that had belonged to our Aunt Rebekah, our mother's closest friend in childhood.

"Rebekah has your beauty, Rachel, and your brilliance, Leah," she would say. "Perhaps one day you will meet her."

I felt like responding, "Please, just once, tell me that I am also smart." I did not have the courage, though, to speak my true feelings.

Our village of Nahor was built around a large, central courtyard. Nearly all our relatives lived in the nearby homes. Each morning our cousins Kishar and

Zaltu stood in the courtyard and called out for me. I joined them to herd sheep and goats from our family's flock. Leah stayed at home and worked alongside our elderly aunts, weaving, spinning yarn, and making perfumes and lotions.

Kishar and Zaltu, both older than me, called me their apprentice and gave me the most difficult chores: drawing water, searching for lost lambs, and bringing the flock back together at the day's end. I did not mind, for I thrived on hiking and chasing sheep in the desert sun. When I grew tired, I sat with my cousins. Just a few moons shy of nine years old, I listened wide-eyed as they talked. They spoke of the boys to whom they were promised and giggled about how to please their grooms on their wedding nights.

"Rachel," said Kishar. "Your eyes and complexion are exquisite. If your breasts grow large and your waist grows thin, you will capture a handsome husband and have a wedding night full of passion."

I blushed and responded quietly, "I am more than my appearance. I want to be appreciated for my personality, not only for my looks."

I looked at Zaltu. She pursed her mouth tight to keep from laughing.

Each evening when we returned home, Leah was often waiting at the door to greet us. Kishar and Zaltu acknowledged Leah only long enough to insist that she give them perfume for their wrists and necks. From listening to our cousins all day, I knew that they snuck out at night to meet their betrothed and did not want to smell like sheep. I complained to our mother that Kishar and Zaltu treated Leah poorly and gave me the hardest tasks.

My mother put her arm around me and said, "Remember what their names mean. In the stories of the gods, Kishar's parents are serpents and Zaltu is the goddess of strife. Let them teach you to herd sheep. You need them for nothing more."

One night, I awoke to a sound in the courtyard. I peered out our window and saw the outline of a couple sitting in the moonlight. I assumed it was either Kishar or Zaltu and her betrothed. Then I heard their voices. The couple was my father and mother, arguing.

"Can you at least appreciate my efforts?" said my father. "I have tried, but cannot find a groom for her."

"Laban, even though her eyes might scare some men, we cannot give up and say that she will never marry," replied our mother. "Do you want Leah to grow old and childless in our home?"

"Do you think I want to be responsible for her forever?" my father exclaimed. "I have approached every shepherd and farmer in our valley. Today, I even spoke to that poor widower who grows chickpeas on the valley's edge."

"But he is almost your age, Laban," gasped my mother. "Besides, he can hardly feed his own family."

"You need not worry," answered my father. "Like the other men, he believes Leah will bring the night demon Lilith into his home."

"Could you not offer a more generous dowry?" my mother said anxiously. "Perhaps a little wealth might convince a potential suitor."

My father retorted, "We could marry Rachel off to a wealthy merchant, while a bricklayer might not even have Leah as a third wife."

I pictured Leah growing old in my parents' house, and I worried about her future. I was angry that potential suitors would judge Leah solely on her appearance. Likewise, I did not want a husband who married me only because of my beauty. The next morning, though, I said nothing to Leah about what I had overheard.

After the sheep-shearing season, the tax collector made his yearly trek to our village. He was a short, jovial man who lived in Haran but traveled to all the surrounding villages. Although my father loathed parting with any of his wealth, he always invited the tax collector to join us for dinner. After a few cups of barley beer, the tax collector happily repeated all the news and gossip he had heard during his recent travels.

"Who else knows more about our neighbors?" reasoned my father.

The tax collector told my father about a medicine woman who had recently settled in Haran and was reputed to be in favor with the gods. The next morning, my mother begged my father to let the medicine woman examine Leah. My father reluctantly agreed to let her and Leah go and even gave up a mangy goat for payment. I did not want to miss the opportunity to go to the city. I had been to Haran only twice before, when our father brought fleece and wool to sell.

"Please, Mother, may I go with you and Leah to Haran?" I asked. "I will not be a bother."

Our mother, worried about Leah, was in no mood to argue. She sighed and told me that I could join them. As the sun rose midway through the sky, we left for Haran.

Before our feet had time to grow tired, the walls of the city rose in front of us. We walked through the city's main gate, arriving at the edge of the market. I had forgotten how the city smelled like a mixture of fresh fish, roasted lamb, and strong incense. We wandered through the narrow alleys, trying to remember the tax collector's directions. We passed stalls selling copper jewelry, sandals, clay bowls, spices, and fresh meats. Finally, we located Rafaela in a squalid back corner of the market.

"You have come to see the medicine woman?" she asked with a dubious grin. We nodded and she continued, "I am Rafaela, the woman whom you seek."

I felt fearful for Leah as our mother pushed her forward, saying, "Her eyes, we were hoping…"

Rafaela lifted Leah's veil, looked into her eyes, and grunted, "There is a cure."

She called to a young girl playing in the dirt and said, "Come, Zilpah. We have a customer."

Rafaela's stall was filled with hundreds of glass bottles and clay bowls. I struggled to identify the contents of the containers, spotting carob pods, figs, pomegranates, almond branches, seashells, and olive oil. Rafaela asked Leah to lie down on a high table at the center of the stall. Her daughter scurried beneath the table and sat in the dust.

She lifted up bottles and jars, peering at their contents. If the contents pleased her, she smelled the concoction and even put a drop on her tongue to taste it. Finally she settled on a pink glass bottle filled with a cloudy ointment. She dabbed the ointment into Leah's eyes. Leah winced, and tears flowed down her cheeks. Rafaela gave Leah a small idol with large round eyes and told her to hold it tight against her chest. Then Rafaela closed her eyes. Swaying, she mumbled to the beat of her body's movement, "Noble Inanna, darling of the goddesses, torch of heaven and earth, radiance of the world. Wipe the sin from this girl's eyes. I know not her wrongdoing, but she is just a youth. Have mercy on her. Accept her repentance. May she be clothed with beauty, like the rising moonlight."

Rafaela repeated this prayer many times, growing increasingly shrill and swaying more frantically with each repetition. At last, she was finished. Wiping sweat from her forehead, she demanded the goat as payment. Zilpah climbed out from under the table and struggled to push the goat out of the back of the stall. Rafaela handed the ointment and the wide-eyed idol to Leah to bring home.

As we left, the bustle of the market quickly surrounded us. Once we were out of Rafaela's view, our mother stopped to examine Leah's eyes. They certainly looked no different to me. Our mother weakly claimed that she saw an improvement.

"May I also get an idol before we go home?" I asked my mother. To soften the request, I added, "Then Leah and I can pray together."

Our mother looked too disappointed about Leah's eyes to protest. She took Leah and me by the hands and began to walk. I thought that we were wandering aimlessly, but we arrived at a large idol workshop.

"I believe that your great, great grandfather Terah once owned this workshop," my mother said.

She let me choose an *asherah*, a small figurine with curved hips and large breasts. All the women who I knew prayed to *asherahs* for hips strong enough to birth many babies and breasts full enough to feed them. I giggled at my new *asherah*'s exaggerated figure, which I found both absurd and enticing. My mother paid the merchant a few copper coins. I held my *asherah* up and compared it to Leah's wide-eyed idol.

"My *asherah* is beautiful, don't you think?" I said.

When Leah did not answer, I realized that I should not have said anything.

We proudly showed our idols to our father when we returned home. Our father prayed only to his idol of Dumuzi, whom he called a manly god. His Dumuzi idol sat at the center of our house. Our mother prayed to a small *asherah*. Intricately carved and smoothly polished out of stone, our mother's *asherah* bore a striking resemblance to her. My clay *asherah*, which had looked so beautiful in the market, looked plain in comparison. Leah and I placed our new idols among the perfume bottles in our room. Although we told our parents that we prayed to them, we mostly held them in our hands, looked at their shapely bodies, and made up stories about their adventures.

The night that we returned from Haran, I heard muffled crying from Leah's bed. "Leah, are you all right?" I whispered.

"Rachel, what is my sin?" she replied.

"I heard Rafaela's prayer also," I said. "I do not understand it. I cannot remember you ever committing a wrongdoing, let alone one so terrible that the gods would punish you. You and I argue sometimes, but usually I am equally to blame. You even treat our elderly aunties politely when they get bossy."

When Rafaela's ointment failed to help her eyes, Leah began making her own medicines. Since Leah could not go outside, she directed my mother and me to collect ingredients—aloe, figs, balm, different flowers, and berries. Every concoction that Leah created either irritated her eyes or did nothing.

"Leah," I said, to lift her spirits, "just remember how beautiful your eyes look in the morning."

"You are a little girl who does not understand adult beauty," Leah snapped.

I looked at the ground in shame.

Leah laughed at me. For the first time, her laugh was full of envy. She said, "Don't worry, Rachel. You are the beautiful one."

Envy has an ugly sound.

Leah was right. Another sheep-shearing season passed, and my body began to change. My waist grew thin and my chest and hips swelled out. I spent so much time outside that my skin always had a deep bronze glow like glazed clay. I began to notice that people, especially boys, turned when I walked by. At first, I enjoyed the attention. But when the tax collector came for his yearly visit, his eyes followed me as I served beer and made me feel immodest. Three shepherd boys from Haran, who pastured their flocks in our valley, began calling me "Asherah." Soon, boys from our village heard their taunts and began calling me "Asherah" as well. I told my mother about the tax collector's wandering eyes and the boy's taunts.

She responded "You should thank the gods for having such a problem."

"I am thankful for my looks," I responded. "It is just that I worry that boys only appreciate me for my appearance and nothing else."

"You know that is not true," my mother said.

Kishar and Zaltu laughed when boys called me "Asherah." "Those boys are only flirting," said Zaltu. "You need to learn to flirt back."

I was relieved when Kishar and Zaltu finally got married. By fall, both were pregnant and stopped herding. My father entrusted me to shepherd sheep from our family's flock on my own. I only missed Kishar and Zaltu when I brought the sheep to the village well in the evening. Without their help, I could not remove the stone lid from the well. I had to rely on the shepherd boys or my brothers to move it for me.

As they pushed the stone, they mocked, "Do you like our muscles, Asherah?"

One evening, as I approached the well, I noticed a young man whom I never had seen before. As soon as he saw me, he single-handedly moved the stone cover from the well.

"He is showing off for you, Asherah," the shepherd boys from Haran called out. "This stranger has been asking for you."

Before I knew it, the stranger grabbed me and planted a kiss firmly on my cheek. The boys started hooting and clapping. I felt my face grow flushed.

Just as I began to run away, the stranger called out, "I am Jacob, your cousin. My mother Rebekah, your father's sister, sent me. I meant no offense. I am just so pleased to see you."

I stopped to look over my shoulder. The family resemblance was clear. Jacob's face reflected my father's features, while his complexion matched Leah's skin tone. I had heard the name "Jacob" before. Every few years, Aunt Rebekah sent a servant to our village to collect news of our family. When the servant arrived, excitement filled our home. The last servant who visited had said Jacob was intelligent and clever. The servant described Rebekah's other son, Esau, as having a dull mind and crude friends. I was glad that Jacob, and not Esau, had come to visit. I imagined Esau calling me "Asherah" with the shepherd boys.

I took Jacob's hand and started herding the flock quickly back to my family's house. I left Jacob by the door and ran inside. Out of breath, I found our father praying to his idol of Dumuzi. I spoke so quickly that my father had to tell me to slow down.

Taking a deep breath, I said, "Jacob, your nephew, my cousin, Rebekah's younger son, has arrived for a visit."

"Jacob, here?!" my father exclaimed, and ran out to greet him.

Our mother declared Jacob to be the spitting image of Aunt Rebekah. Jacob was short and muscular with smooth skin and thick dark curls on his head. Leah looked him up and down, but did not speak. She seemed to decide that he would not be interested in her. Perhaps she was right. Jacob hardly acknowledged Leah's presence.

Leah and I helped our mother quickly prepare a feast while our father ran to the nearby homes to announce Jacob's arrival. He invited our uncles and their sons to the celebration. As we served the food, Jacob told his story. He described how he had tricked Esau out of both his birthright and his blessing. As the first born son, Esau had been destined to inherit his father's wealth and blessing as the next family elder. When Jacob told how Esau traded his birthright for a bowl of lentil soup, my father began to laugh.

"Was it as easy to convince Esau to give up his blessing?" asked my father, chuckling.

"My father is almost blind. With my mother's help, I dressed up as Esau and tricked my father into blessing me instead," Jacob said. "My father did not know the difference until it was too late."

As Jacob explained it, Esau was physical and strong, but impulsive and not too intelligent. Still, I could not help feeling sorry for Esau. I especially felt bad for blind Uncle Isaac, whom Jacob had also tricked.

Then Jacob spoke about Rebekah. "My mother taught me well," said Jacob. "From her, I learned that the God of Sarah and Abraham created heaven and earth, forming men and women in the Divine Image. Just as it is here, in your village of Nahor, the God of Sarah and Abraham remains my parents' patron God."

My father sat up stiffly and snapped, "Jacob, your mother started with this nonsense about Abraham's god before she left our parents' home. I thought that she might grow wiser with time, but apparently she is still foolish. Nobody in our village has prayed to the God of Sarah and Abraham since my grandmother Milcah died. My sons and I pray to our idols, not to some god that you cannot see."

"The God of Sarah and Abraham is no longer your patron?" asked Jacob with surprise.

He looked around the room at my relatives' blank faces and then noticed my parents' idols.

Drawing a deep breath, Jacob said, "Those idols are just clay and stone. They have no power. Humans like you and me created them. But the one God created us. Praying to such idols is simple folly, Uncle Laban. That large idol has less power than a donkey."

I had never heard anybody speak to our father so rudely, especially in front of our family. It no longer surprised me that Jacob had tricked his own father. My cousin seemed smart and certainly committed to this god of his, but he was also full of self-importance. I looked over at Leah and saw that she was smiling. She was enjoying this argument between our father and our newly found cousin.

Later, back in our room, Leah said, "Jacob made a lot of sense. Maybe I do not resemble an *asherah* like you, Rachel, but I still have God within me."

Leah's happiness was short-lived. Although Leah and Jacob talked end-lessly in the following days about the powerlessness of idols, Jacob made it obvi-ous that he favored me. He said that God could be seen in all people, but that he saw more of God in me. My mother told me to accept Jacob's words as a compliment. But to me, being called the "Divine Image" sounded little better than "asherah."

After one moon's time, Jacob told my father that he loved me and offered to work seven years in exchange for my hand in marriage. My father, although disturbed by Jacob's religious devotions, agreed to our union. Jacob was family. Our flocks were growing larger. Our brothers had recently given up herding sheep to become wheat farmers. My father could use Jacob's help.

"Better that I give Rachel to you than to an outsider," my father told Jacob.

I wish I could say that I loved Jacob from the beginning or that I looked forward to our wedding day as much as he did. Neither statement would be true. Jacob was loving and kind to me. For that, I was thankful. At the same time, I found it difficult to return his admiration and affection. We had very little in common. I loved to be outdoors herding sheep. Jacob had to work with the flocks all day, but much preferred to stay in our village and talk about his beliefs.

During the seven years leading up to my marriage to Jacob, I tried to avoid thinking about my future. I focused on developing my skills as a shep-herdess. I learned to recognize the first signs of illness in a sheep or goat. Many nights I stayed up until dawn, tending to ewes giving birth. I could look at a lamb and tell if it had the personality to get into mischief. With hand signals and whistles I drove the flock to pasture. At the end of the day, I circled the flock until they gathered together.

"Rachel, I enjoy watching you work," said my mother. "You appear to herd the flock effortlessly, but your firm muscles and the concentration on your face tell a different story."

My reputation as a shepherdess extended beyond our valley. I entered herd-ing competitions at the yearly sheep-shearing festival in Haran, and I usually won. Finally, I was known for something other than my beauty. Our father arranged for me to have my own apprentice, a young girl named Bilhah, the daughter of the widowed chickpea farmer. She was sweet, strong, and conscientious, and soon she pledged herself as a maidservant to our family. I appreciated her companionship. She made me laugh when she teased the village boys.

My father forbade Jacob and me from being alone together when we herded sheep. "You wait your seven years," my father told him. "Only then can you be alone with Rachel."

Once Bilhah became my apprentice, she went with me into the pastures. Since I was no longer alone, Jacob felt that he could join our flocks together and go to pasture with us. Jacob called Bilhah our "chaperone." His skills as a shepherd were sloppy, and he could handle only a small flock on his own. He distracted me with his annoying chatter about the "true God." If I offered any suggestions about herding, he became temperamental.

He told me, "Bilhah is your apprentice, Rachel, not me. I came to talk, not to learn to shepherd."

At home, I often found Jacob and Leah deep in conversation. Sometimes I tried to join in, but they spoke mostly about the God of Sarah and Abraham, and I quickly became bored. I envied how Jacob and Leah enjoyed each other's company. I enjoyed listening only when Leah spoke about her experiments with different healing potions. Although she had not discovered a cure for her own eyes, Leah had created a powerful mandrake root formula for sheep. When my father fed Leah's potion to the ewes, they gave birth to larger, stronger lambs.

I began hearing other shepherds talk about Leah as a medicine woman. The shepherds said that Leah's healing power was even stronger than that of the medicine woman Rafaela from Haran. One evening, Rafaela appeared at our door unannounced. Her daughter Zilpah stood behind her, looking at the ground. She begged our father to take Zilpah as an apprentice to Leah. Leah sat silently and smiled to herself. When my father looked at Leah for approval, she nodded.

"I will use her to collect herbs and plants for me," said Leah. "No longer will I bother Rachel or our mother with such menial work. I will enjoy having a servant."

Seven years had seemed like a long time when Jacob and I first became engaged. All too soon, our wedding loomed only a few weeks away, and still my heart did not beat quickly when I thought of Jacob. I resigned myself to marrying a man for whom I felt little affection. With no prospects for marriage herself, Leah began to sulk as the wedding drew nearer. Being self-absorbed with my own doubts, I hardly noticed Leah's ongoing infatuation with Jacob.

The day before the wedding, I said bitterly to Leah, "I do not love Jacob. He is too outspoken and arrogant. I fear that he loves me only for my appearance. Even worse, I am bored when he talks about his faith. I will have a loveless marriage, Leah."

Leah's face displayed a mixture of envy with anger. I immediately realized that I should not have spoken. It was cruel to push my complaints about my betrothal in her face.

She said, "Rachel, I do not think you know how lucky you are. You are marrying a man with such intelligence and conviction. I would give anything to be in your place."

Then I made a statement that would change both of our lives.

"Leah," I said, "You should marry Jacob in my place. You have much more in common with him than I do. You can wear my veil. He will not know the difference until it is too late."

Leah sat stunned at my suggestion. "You should not joke about something so important. You are only nervous about the wedding," she said.

Shaking my head, I said, "No, Leah, I am not joking. I do not want to marry Jacob."

Leah thought for a moment. Then she said, "Perhaps it is not such a bad idea."

We had no difficulty convincing my father of the plan. I could see his mind work. He liked to scheme. He could marry Leah off to Jacob. With my looks, I would have no problem finding another husband. As we spoke to our father, my mother sat silently. I knew that she disapproved. I tried not to look at her.

The evening of the wedding, I heard the festivities in the distance. I passed the time reorganizing Leah's and my room. Earlier in the day, she had moved into a small house built for Jacob and me on the opposite side of the courtyard from our parents' home. I smiled at the sudden freedom that my life held. I had escaped a marriage that I did not want and, at the same time, brought great happiness into Leah's life. Certainly, in time, Jacob would realize that he had married the right sister for him.

The morning after the wedding, I heard Jacob shouting with rage in the courtyard.

Leah climbed up our ladder. "My husband hates me," she cried. "What have I done? How could I have been so stupid? He wants a wife that looks like an *asherah*, not me. Rachel, Jacob is demanding you."

As I tried to calm Leah down, we overheard Jacob arguing with our father. I was hugging Leah when we both heard what our future would be.

My father calmly explained, "It is not our practice to marry off the younger daughter before the older. Wait until the bridal week is over and you can marry Rachel also, provided you serve me another seven years." And we heard Jacob grumble his acceptance of this scheme.

Leah gasped. I sat in shock. I did not want to believe that our father could be so cruel.

Leah untangled herself from my arms and stood up. We looked at one another. I wanted to reassure Leah, but I could not find the words. I opened my mouth in silence.

Leah cried, "You are now my rival." She began climbing down the ladder.

"Leah," I called out. "Do not let our father and Jacob make enemies out of us. We have both been tricked."

But Leah was gone. She isolated herself in her new house. She refused to see anybody but Zilpah, not even our mother. I wanted to comfort her but knew better than to visit.

"How can I get married now?" I asked my mother. "Leah will not even talk to me. I cannot imagine my wedding without her."

"I know it is difficult," our mother answered. "In time, Leah will forgive you."

"Forgive me?" I responded. "She plotted with me. Our father tricked not only Jacob, but both of us as well. I do not love Jacob, and I cannot make him love Leah."

"I understand," my mother said quietly. "But you must honor your father. You cannot break his agreement with Jacob."

I did honor my father's agreement, despite my anger. Just a week after Leah's wedding, I also married Jacob. Still enraged from having been duped, Jacob was aloof and irritable on our wedding night. He insisted that I remove Leah's and my idols from our home. I picked up Leah's wide-eyed idol and realized its arms had been broken. I brought my *asherah* and Leah's broken idol to my parents' home, putting them next to our mother's *asherah*.

Without telling Jacob, I visited our idols often at our parents' home. I went in the early evening, when Jacob thought that I was still herding the flock. I would gaze at the idols and ask them to bring Leah and me back together. I missed my sister. Even though we saw each other every day, we rarely talked. Zilpah and Bilhah communicated for us.

Years passed, and Leah gave birth to one son after another while I remained barren. When Leah gave birth to her first son, I hoped that Jacob might pay her more attention and leave me alone. When she gave birth again, I wondered when I might have a child. When Leah proudly nursed her third and, then, fourth sons, I began to worry.

"Pray to the idols for a child," my mother would tell me.

"Mother, I do pray for a child. I pray to the idols and I pray to the God of Sarah and Abraham," I said. "I no longer believe that either will help me."

"Why, then, do you return so often to the idols?" my mother asked.

"Our three idols make me feel close to you and Leah," I said. "They remind me of how we used to giggle and laugh together when Leah and I were girls."

Jacob spent most nights in my bedroom, visiting Leah only once or twice every moon cycle. Even so, Leah had four sons, and I still had none. For the first time in my life, I knew envy. I pictured Rafaela telling Leah to repent for her sins, and I imagined that Rafaela had spoken to me instead. I fought melancholy. One evening, I could no longer contain my emotions.

I cried to Jacob in despair as we lay in bed, "Give me children or I shall die."

Jacob looked at me in shock, then pity. He finally said, "Can I take the place of God, who has denied you children?"

I did not respond. I no longer had faith in my parents' idols or in Jacob's God. The next morning, I told Jacob to take Bilhah as a concubine. Bilhah agreed easily, smiling as Jacob led her to my bedroom. Together, they had two sons, Dan and Naphtali. Bilhah's boys, though, did not fulfill my yearnings for a child. Leah still viewed me as her rival and, to stay even, she gave Zilpah to Jacob. Zilpah gave birth to twin boys. Our house was filled with children, but none were mine.

Finally I swallowed my pride and went to Leah. I had long suspected that Leah made fertility potions not only for sheep, but for herself as well. Leah even had her oldest son, Reuben, collecting mandrakes for her now. Softly, I knocked on Leah's door. She ushered me into her bedroom. My voice quivering, I asked her for a fertility potion.

Leah replied coldly, "Was it not enough for you to take away my husband, that you would also take the mandrakes my son has collected?"

"Please, Leah, give me your potion," I pleaded. "You can have an extra night of romance with Jacob in return."

Leah stared at me and said sharply, "I do not need your pity to earn a night with Jacob."

"Leah," I continued. "If you still believe we have a rivalry, then you have prevailed. You have given four children to Jacob. I do not want a child for Jacob. I just want to be a mother. I have watched you with your sons, and I am envious."

"You envy me?" Leah asked.

"Yes, I do, Leah," I responded.

Leah stood for a moment before pulling a blue glass bottle off her shelf.

"Take this potion each morning," she said. "It has worked well for me." She smiled slightly as she passed me the bottle.

Still I did not become pregnant. Leah had two more sons and a daughter, who she named Dinah. I prayed to the idols in my parents' home. I prayed to the God of Sarah and Abraham. I took Leah's potion. When the bottle ran empty, Leah gave me more. The first time she poured more potion into my bottle, a tense silence filled her room. The second time, she looked at me with sympathy and wished me luck. The third time, Leah hugged me and whispered that she prayed for me.

Then, one moon, my period of women did not come. A second and a third moon passed. My belly began to swell. Finally, I too was pregnant. I asked both my mother and Leah to attend to the birth. They took turns holding my hand during the long labor. I gave birth to a son and named him Joseph.

As I cradled Joseph, I said, "My disgrace has been taken away." Jacob, tired of his long servitude and our father's trickery, decided that we should return to the land of his birth He spoke passionately about fulfilling his family's legacy.

"We must return to the land that God gave my grandfather and grandmother," Jacob said, as Leah enthusiastically nodded her head in agreement.

This "legacy" meant very little to me but I wanted desperately to escape our father's clutches. I saw our father only as a trickster who had taken advantage of our hard work. Jacob, Leah, and I had labored for years to build up our father's flock. But our father kept almost all the sheep and goats for himself, treating us like servants. To leave for our new home with the wealth owed to us, the three of us created a scheme of our own. Jacob asked our father permission to take with us only the dark-colored sheep and the speckled and spotted goats — which were the rarest in the flock. For many moons, we worked secretively. With Leah's knowledge of mandrakes and my knowledge of sheep and goats, we made sure that only dark-colored lambs and speckled and spotted goat kids were born.

Our father grew furious when he realized he had been duped. He accused Jacob of trickery and theft. He told Leah and me that we were traitors.

"We learned to scheme from you, father," Leah answered him.

"Please do not yell at us in front of the children," I added, calmly and deliberately.

Jacob told us to prepare in secret to leave our village. He feared that our father was angry enough to prevent us from leaving with him.

On the night before we left, I went to my parents' home to visit the idols for a final time. My mother saw me touching each figurine. She sensed that I would be leaving.

She lifted up her *asherah* and handed it to me. "Take this *asherah* with you, my daughter, for I know it resembles me," she said. "It will bring me joy to know that I am always with you. Take also Leah's broken idol. Let it always remind you to cherish your relationship with your sister. Do not let it break again. I will keep your *asherah*. When I pray, you will be with me."

"I treasure your beautiful *asherah*," I said, hugging my mother good-bye.

Rachel takes the idols and places them in Lilith's ark. Then she passes the ark to her sister, Leah. "We share the same tale, my sister," Rachel says, "though our stories and gifts are different."

6 | LEAH: A ROOT OF A MANDRAKE

A HINT FROM TORAH:

Once, at the time of the wheat harvest,
Reuben came upon some mandrakes in the field
and brought them to his mother Leah. GENESIS 30:1

The matriarch Leah bears six sons and one daughter in hopes
of capturing Jacob's love. The name Leah means "weary." Leah's
unrequited love for Jacob and her escalating rivalry with Rachel
undoubtedly left her weary. Still, the Torah hints at an aspect of
Leah's life beyond being a mother and an unloved wife. In the
ancient world, medicine women and faith healers brewed potions
to cure barrenness and promote fertility. Mandrakes especially
were believed to have mysterious powers. In the Torah, Leah's
son Reuben brings mandrakes to her. Rachel begs Leah for
them to cure her barrenness. In this chapter's midrash, Reuben's
mandrakes are not the first that Leah has used in creating a
fertility potion.

Let us meet Leah...

My parents' home was my prison as a young girl. Its stone foundation and clay brick walls confined me. If I ventured outside its dark rooms, the sun and sand quickly irritated my eyes so that I could hardly see. My mother warned me that I might go blind and forbade me from going outside in sun or wind without a thick wool veil over my face. Girls my age did not wear veils, so this marked me as a misfit. Whenever I wore the veil, I shuffled hesitantly like an old woman. I prayed for cloudy, windless days—the only days when my mother permitted me to do chores in our courtyard without my veil. I understood my mother's rules. Still, I dreamt of tearing the veil off my face.

It was in our courtyard that I learned that I looked grotesque. On one mild, cloudy day, when I was a few moons shy of 10, I ventured outside with my eyes uncovered. Young cousins of mine chased one another in a game of tag. I sat down to watch. One little cousin saw me and shrieked. Her twin brother gawked and then asked if the night demon Lilith had captured my eyes. Stunned by his words, I said nothing. The boy asked whether Lilith had taken possession of my tongue as well. That night, I told Rachel about the boy.

"His elder brothers have spread lies about Lilith possessing your eyes. He is simply repeating their gossip," said Rachel.

"My own cousins believe that a night demon distorted my face?" I asked, my voice rising.

"I thought you knew, for all the boys talk about it," Rachel answered. "There is no truth to their story."

After that, I often dreamt of Lilith poking my eyes with a stick and stealing them. When I awoke, I frantically felt my eye sockets to check if they were empty. I grabbed for the copper-faced mirror that rested by my bedside and, to calm my heart, I gazed at my eyes, which were clear only right after I awoke. After sleep, my eyes had a lovely sparkle, like freshly washed grapes. Each morning, I prayed that my eyes might stay forever clear and focused. Once I had dressed, I would peer in the mirror again, hoping that my deformity had vanished. My eyes stared back at me like two rotten apricots. My mother told me that my eyes were not nearly as repulsive as I imagined, but I did not believe her. I saw how people looked at me, and I knew.

I tried not to resent Rachel, for I needed her. She was my only link beyond the courtyard. Nobody else my age talked to me. Every night, as we lay in our beds, Rachel retold each detail of our older cousins' conversations, the village boys' antics, and the shepherds' gossip by the village well. It was difficult not to be envious. Rachel was bronze-skinned and muscular from herding sheep. My skin remained pale, and my body jiggled like my elderly aunties' arms. Rachel smiled and giggled, eternally cheerful. Her good fortune irked me.

My daily companions were three elderly aunties with whom I worked. Their conversations bored me, for they either complained of their aching backs or talked about husbands long dead. The auntie whose knees popped every time she sat down taught me to weave. When her arms grew weak, I ran the shuttle through the warp for her.

My second auntie, whose crude jokes made me blush, taught me to use a drop spindle to turn fleece into yarn. When she completed a batch of fleece, she wrapped the yarn around my two outstretched arms to form a skein. These two aunts were sisters; they entertained each other by arguing.

I spent most of my days with the third auntie, who was blind. I found comfort in knowing that she could not see my face. This aunt mixed sweet-smelling perfumes and lotions. She taught me to create fragrant oils by cold-pressing fruit peels and steam-distilling flowers. She showed me how to mix frankincense and other spices with olive oil. My mother bought us cinnamon and calamus at the market in Haran, and my auntie taught me how just a pinch of either could perfect a perfume. Before long, my skills surpassed hers. She smiled proudly when the women of our village brought glass canisters to fill with my perfumes.

"Listen not to the taunts of your cousins," this kind auntie told me. "You have gifts for our world, a keen sense of smell and a bright mind. The gods have plans for you."

I prayed that the gods would reveal the purpose of my deformity, but they did not answer. As my hips grew wider and my breasts larger, I worried that my auntie was wrong. Perhaps the gods had forgotten about me. By my age, most girls were betrothed for marriage. My parents never spoke of finding a husband for me. I imagined the humiliation of forever remaining an unwed prisoner in my parents' home. On the day that my periods of women began, I found the courage to talk to my mother.

"The goddess Inanna has visited me, and my periods of women have begun," I told her. "Has my father arranged for my betrothal?"

My mother hugged me and wept.

"He has been searching, Leah," my mother said. "Truthfully, your eyes have scared some suitors, but I know that there is a young man waiting for you. You are smart and talented. Somebody very lucky will marry you, my daughter."

One moon later, the tax collector came to our village for his yearly visit. He frowned at my eyes, then told my father and mother about a medicine woman in Haran named Rafaela.

"She has done miracles with even worse cases than your daughter," he said.

The next morning, my father agreed to let my mother take me to find this medicine woman. Rachel pestered and sulked until our mother said that she could come with us.

With a veil over my face, I struggled to walk. I heard Rachel run ahead, then back, chasing the goat that we brought for the medicine woman. If I peered downward, I saw her shadow flutter like a butterfly. Her laughter annoyed me. I resented that our journey was simply an adventure to her. When we entered the market in Haran, crowds of people bumped and jostled me. I worked to steady myself under the veil and clutched my mother's hand tightly. Aromatic smells enticed me as we passed stalls of spices, but I fought the urge to stop for ingredients for my perfumes. I wanted to find the medicine woman and end my ordeal.

As we walked more deeply into the market's center, we stopped several people to ask for directions. Finally, an elderly man peeling fruit pointed to a stall hidden behind a violet wool curtain. Nervous and curious, I lifted my veil to look. A plump woman sat on a stool in front of the stall, picking at her fingernails. Around her neck, she wore a large stone amulet to ward off evil spirits. When she saw us approach, she stood up and dusted the sand off her tunic.

My heart beat quickly as Rafaela lifted my veil and declared that she had a cure for my eyes. Shooing her small daughter ahead of her and ushering us into her stall, she commanded me to lie down on a table. The sounds of the market had faded. When Rafaela pulled my eyes wide open, I saw grime and dirt stuck in her fingernails.

"This is very difficult," she said with a grunt. "I will try."

She jabbed ointment into the corner of each eye. My eyes immediately clenched shut and began to water profusely.

"Your tears are a good sign," said Rafaela. "The ointment is clearing away your misdeeds. The goddess Inanna feels your repentance. Do not wipe away your tears. They must flow freely."

I felt her press a clay figure into my hands, telling me to hold it to my chest. Then Rafaela began a chanting a repetitive prayer. With growing fervency and rising pitch, she pleaded with the goddess Inanna to forgive my sins and cure my deformity. Over and over again, I heard the words sin, wrongdoing, and repentance.

Questions flooded my mind. What sin? What terrible act had I committed to deserve my grotesque eyes? If I did not know my wrongdoing, how could I repent?

When at last it was over, I heard Rafaela demand that my mother pay her. Gradually, my eyes opened and I felt my right eye still staring up in its socket. Dimly, I saw that I held a wide-eyed idol. Rafaela told me to keep it, and pressed the bottle of ointment into my hands as well. I asked her what was in it, but she only said coyly, "A medicine woman never shares her secrets."

After we left Rafaela's stall, I smelled the ointment and my suspicion was confirmed. It was nothing more than sesame oil and aloe. I could have made it myself. On our way back through Haran, we stopped and bought an *asherah* for Rachel, as I had a new idol. Rachel could not resist pointing out how beautiful her idol was. I pretended not to hear her.

Although Rafaela's ointment did not help heal my eyes, her words haunted me for many moons. That night and for many nights afterward, I slept feverishly. I dreamt that the gods dragged me to a heavenly court. A pair of identical goddesses turned away when they saw me approach. Dumuzi, my father's patron god, convicted me without hearing any testimony. I begged him to reveal my sin, but he refused. For my punishment, Lilith flew down and stole my eyes.

She shrieked, "I will return your eyes when you fulfill your purpose."

"What purpose? Tell me what to do," I cried. She laughed and flew away.

Some nights, Lilith's voice sounded like Rafaela's. Other nights, her voice sounded like Rachel's. One night, Lilith's voice sounded like my mother's. I awoke sweaty, but oddly serene. I had a plan. Rafaela's stall had been lined with potions, most of which I could mix on my own. I did not need Rafaela. I could create my own cure for my eyes. That morning, I revealed my plan to my mother and Rachel.

"Leah, you have brilliance while Rachel has beauty," said my mother. I was pleased to see Rachel frown. "The gods gave you a clever mind for a purpose. With their help, you will find success."

I asked Rachel and my mother to gather ingredients for me. Together, they combed our valley. They located a small gathering of shrubs that gave off gummy myrrh. The myrrh stung my eyes, but I used it make a salve for blemishes on my mother's face. They collected aloe plants. I made a balm for my father's rough and cracking hands. From wheat flour, tree sap, and dried fruit, I found remedies for stomach pains, headaches, and sores. None of my concoctions cured my own deformity. My mother said that I had found my calling, creating remedies from herbs and plants. I disagreed with her. I desperately desired to be betrothed for marriage. Even more, I sought a cure for my eyes. I had accomplished neither. When Rachel's periods of women began, she asked me for a potion to lessen her cramps. As I handed her a vial, I realized that she was no longer a girl. She had grown shapely and stunning. Any wealthy shepherd or merchant would beg my father for her hand in marriage.

That evening, Rachel confided in me, "Shepherd boys from our village and Haran call me "Asherah." Our brothers do nothing to stop them. Their taunts make me feel immodest."

"You do look divine," I snapped back. "You should be thankful."

"Please, do not be like those boys, Leah," Rachel answered, her voice cracking. "I hope that at least you, my sister, would appreciate me for more than my appearance."

I had no sympathy for Rachel's complaints. The very next day, our cousin Jacob arrived in our village. When I saw Jacob for the first time, I was sweaty from boiling figs and mashing them into a balm. My hands and tunic were covered with sticky pieces of boiled fruit. When I greeted Jacob, he could not hide a grimace of disgust.

I tried not to blame Jacob for recoiling from me. His reaction was only too familiar. My cousins had always reacted in the same manner. But as I listened carefully to Jacob's words as he spoke, I realized that he was not like my other cousins. Jacob did not pray to idols. He believed in an all-powerful but invisible God. He preached that this God of Sarah and Abraham had put a spark of divinity in each of us. My father instantly disapproved of Jacob's beliefs. I did not care. I had prayed to my father's idols, and his gods had not helped me. They only terrified me in my dreams.

My father asked Jacob to stay with us as a shepherd, for he needed help with the flocks. My father set only one condition: Jacob could not speak about the God of Sarah and Abraham in our home. Jacob agreed—then sat outside in the courtyard every evening, talking about his beliefs to anybody who would listen. At first, many of my relatives came to hear Jacob. Before even one moon ended, they had lost interest. I was the only person who sought Jacob out. We sat under a sycamore tree. When the wind blew, I wore a veil. I craved Jacob's attention. I asked him question after question about his beliefs. He told me that my questions made his faith firmer.

"Do you believe in sin?" I asked Jacob one evening.

"I believe that we can make mistakes," Jacob answered. "We can always ask for forgiveness and, if we repent, God allows us another chance."

"Do you think my eyes are God's punishment?" I continued, picturing Lilith holding my eyes.

"God does not punish good people," he answered. "Your eyes reflect God, even if you do not know how."

At that moment, I fell in love with Jacob. After one moon's time, my father gathered our family together. Jacob stood next to my father and brothers, looking proud and eager.

"Our kinsman Jacob, the son of my beloved sister Rebekah, has spent one moon's time in our village. Not only has he proven himself to be an able herdsman, he has fallen in love with one of my daughters," exclaimed my father.

I smiled broadly. My father continued. "Jacob has pledged himself to work for seven years in exchange for Rachel's hand in marriage. I have agreed to their match. May our gods bless Jacob and his betrothed Rachel."

At first, I did not realize that my father said "Rachel" and, foolishly, continued to grin. Only when I saw my family crowd around Rachel did I grasp the reality of my father's words. The shock paralyzed me. My heart felt as though it stopped. Tears welled up in my eyes. A marriage between Jacob and Rachel made no sense. They never spoke, and she complained of his arrogance. Did my conversations with Jacob mean nothing? I looked at Rachel, but she turned away. She knew how I felt about Jacob. Furthermore, my father had broken with tradition and promised the younger sister before the elder. With such an insult, I might never get married. As if she knew my thoughts, my mother put her arm around my shoulder as joyful shouts filled the air.

"Leah, your father and I have not given up hope in finding a match for you. Much can happen in seven years," she whispered. "Do not despair just yet."

Jacob asked to speak, and a hush fell over the family.

"My mother, Rebekah, would wish to celebrate with us today. She sent me to the village of her youth to find a wife. The God of Sarah and Abraham guided me and fulfilled my mission," Jacob said, lifting a wineskin. "I believe that every person reflects a spark of God's presence. But Rachel sparkles twice as brightly as any other girl."

Only after the festivities, Jacob approached me. "Will you congratulate me, Leah?" he asked. "Now, we will be brother and sister, as well as cousins."

"I wish you and your betrothed well," I whispered.

"May I share a story with you? I have spoken about it to nobody," Jacob asked. I nodded slowly, and Jacob continued. "On the first night after I left my parents' home, I found a place to sleep in the desert. I used a simple stone as a pillow. I dreamt intensely. I saw a ladder reaching up to heaven. Angels flew up and down the ladder. I awoke, knowing that I had felt God's presence. When I look at Rachel, I have the same sensation."

For just a moment, I felt grateful that Rachel had found such love. Then I wondered why Jacob had shared this story with me and not her. Jealousy and anger filled my heart. That night, I too dreamt of Jacob's ladder. The angels on the ladder turned on me and told me that I would not wed. They pulled at my hair. I awoke in a panic. Rachel sat on the edge of my bed, stroking my head.

"I could not sleep," Rachel said. "I feel nothing for Jacob. I am not sure that I even like him."

I remained quiet. After a short while, I pretended to fall back to sleep. When I finally did fall asleep, I dreamt of angels pushing me down a ladder. "You are not wanted," the angels called down to me. I heard Lilith screech in the distance.

I tried to avoid Jacob after his betrothal was announced, but he continually sought me out. Late one afternoon, he walked in from my brother's wheat field, carrying two long plant roots in his arms. The roots looked like miniature, contorted humans with long twisted limbs. One root was shaped like a man, and the other, like a woman. "Have you ever seen the root of a mandrake before? They grow as weeds in wheat fields," said Jacob. "In Canaan, medicine women grind these roots and make potions that help ewes have many lambs and cattle have many calves. I know not the recipe, except that these healers mix the female and male roots together."

I held the roots, intrigued by their odd shape and their possible potency.

Jacob continued, "Help me please, Leah. If you create a potion for the ewes in your father's flocks, they will have many lambs. Your father's flocks will grow, and he will look upon me as a true son. Perhaps he will forgive me for my beliefs."

I took the mandrakes from Jacob and retreated to the corner that I used as a workshop. I began by chiseling off a small piece of bark from the female root. I placed the bark into my mouth and began to chew. Sour juices filled my mouth, and I tried not to gag. I felt a rush of energy; then a soft sleepiness filled my body. I fought the urge to nap. I sensed the potential and danger of mandrakes.

I asked Jacob to dig up a complete mandrake plant for me. He returned a short time later covered with dirt. He carried a male root, crowned by several large dark leaves. Its deep yellow fruit had an intense but pleasant smell. I tore one leaf, and it released a putrid odor. Covering my nose, I felt the leaf and knew it would clean sores, if its stench could be lessened.

Over the next several moons, I tried many different preparations of mandrakes. Finally, I settled on a powerful potion made by grinding mandrake roots and fruit together and mixing this pulp with strong wine. Jacob poured my potion into the flock's water troughs during mating season. Soon enough, the ewes gave birth to many healthy, vigorous lambs.

Word of my success spread quickly, and shepherds from neighboring valleys began to visit and ask for my potion. Following my father's instructions, I told them that the potion was a family secret and would not be shared. My father reasoned that a shepherd might marry me to learn its ingredients. During each of the next lambing seasons, shepherds begged for my potion, but none expressed an interest in me as a bride. They considered me a medicine woman, not a potential wife.

Two of my cousins, Zaltu and Kishar, approached me. They had snubbed me as a child. Now they begged for my mandrake potion. They wished to drink it themselves and please their husbands with strong, healthy sons. I had heard rumors that Canaanite women ingested mandrake potions, but I had no reason to help Zaltu and Kishar. I told them that mandrakes would drive them to madness or senility. I gave them a simple perfume of cinnamon and olive oil and told them that I called it "Romance's Scent." They praised my skill and left to share it with their husbands. I giggled at their gullibility.

Jacob, initially enthusiastic about collecting mandrakes, grew tired of the dirty task of uprooting them. My mother was growing older, and it hurt her back to dig up mandrakes. Rachel spent most of her time with the flocks. Even with her new apprentice, Bilhah, she had little time to help me. Besides, I had grown weary of depending on my family.

I told my father that, like Rachel, I needed a maidservant. He grumbled about having to feed another person. The God of Sarah and Abraham must have heard my request. Less than a moon later, Rafaela, the medicine woman, appeared in our village looking haggard and dirty. Her daughter, of whom I had only a faded memory, was now a young woman, walking behind her in tattered clothes. Rafaela begged my father to allow her daughter to become my apprentice and learn to mix potions from me. I asked the daughter for her name.

Avoiding my eyes, she whispered, "Zilpah."

My father and Rafaela agreed that Zilpah would stay as my apprentice for a trial period of one moon.

Although Zilpah seemed dimwitted, I needed the help. I quickly grew to both appreciate Zilpah and be frustrated by her. Although she gave me some independence, she was a daydreamer and easily distracted. If I sent her to collect aloe, she returned with honey. If I told her to gather mandrake roots, she would return with its fruit instead. At least Zilpah is loyal, I told myself. I preferred relying on her rather than asking Rachel for help.

After one moon's time, I asked Zilpah to stay longer as my apprentice. When my father and Zilpah went to Haran to find Rafaela and get her permission, they found her stall empty and abandoned. From the neighboring merchants, they learned that Rafaela had packed up her belongings and left Haran. She had told one merchant that she was moving to Egypt; another that she planned to settle in Ur; and a third, that she was journeying to Canaan. Zilpah had no choice but to pledge herself as my maidservant.

In the year leading up to the wedding, Rachel and I barely spoke. Nearly past the age for marriage myself, I grew increasingly bitter when I looked at

Rachel. She did not appreciate Jacob. Her self-pity angered me. I did not understand the depth of her desperation until the day before her wedding.

Rachel approached me with an irrational plan, a dubious scheme filled
with risk. She wanted me to marry Jacob in her place. The bridal veil, she reasoned, would hide my identity. At first, I thought that Rachel was joking and
was angry at her insensitivity. But then Rachel repeated herself. She truly hoped
to trade places with me. My desire for Jacob and my fear of never marrying
overpowered my good sense. I pushed logic aside and agreed to conspire with
Rachel. When my father quickly agreed to Rachel's plan, I convinced myself
that it would work.

Rachel and I were almost giddy as we planned our deception. I had not
felt so close to her since we were small girls. Our mother refused to participate in our scheme. Only her absence dampened our mood. Together, Rachel
and I went to the river basin and bathed on what would be my wedding day.
As I dipped my head under the cool water, I felt pure even in the midst of
our trickery.

When we returned home, Rachel braided my hair into plaits, forming a
crown around my head. She handed me her favorite perfume, a mix of honey,
oil, and the nectar of desert flowers. I dabbed the perfume on my wrists. Rachel
put my favorite perfume, made from mint and oil, onto her neck. I wore the
family bridal gown, sewn of fine linen by our grandmother Milcah. Rachel
wore the colored tunic intended for me as the bridal attendant. She padded my
chest with fleece to add more shape to my figure. She placed a floor-length
piece of linen over my face and a shorter veil over her own face. The bridal veil
was thick enough to hide my identity, including my deformed eyes. Through it,
I could see only distorted images.

"There is one last detail," said Rachel. "Jacob created a code that he thinks
is romantic. He told it only to me. When you enter the wedding canopy, Jacob will
whisper, 'I am my beloved's.' You must whisper back, 'and my beloved is mine.'"

As the sun began to set, my brothers and male cousins arrived with
Jacob. The girls and women in my family lined the courtyard with lanterns and
began to sing. I came to the door, accompanied by my father and followed by
Rachel. I listened to Rachel's footsteps and realized that she was imitating my
awkward way of walking. By the glow of the lanterns, my father guided me to
the wedding canopy.

I entered the wedding canopy, and Jacob whispered, "I am my beloved's." Timidly I answered, "And my beloved is mine."

I feared that he recognized my voice. A cloud of insecurity enveloped my heart. Through the veil, I glimpsed Jacob's loving gaze. I relished the moment. Nobody had ever looked at me like that before. But my elation faded quickly when I remembered that Jacob believed me to be Rachel. At that moment, I understood. For Jacob, there was no replacement for Rachel. My heart beat with wild shame. I thought that I heard the demons of my dreams laughing at me, but then realized that the laughter came from festive wedding guests. I looked out into the crowd desperately. If I could only find Rachel, perhaps I could signal that our plan was a mistake. I saw her in the distance, walking away from the ceremony toward our home, her stride now light and free.

At the wedding feast, I sat silently between my mother and father. My mother spoke only to the servants and smiled tensely, grinding her teeth. On the other side of my father, Jacob drank wine and laughed with my brothers, uncles, and cousins. Every time Jacob emptied his wine goblet, my father filled it again. When the feast ended, Jacob staggered to our new house, pulling me along with him.

In the darkness of the bedroom, I took off the wedding gown and veil, and silently lay down on the bed. Jacob spoke loving words to Rachel as he kissed and touched me. When Jacob's passion was sated, he fell into a satisfied sleep. I cried through most of the night, my back turned to Jacob. When I finally fell asleep, I dreamt of Lilith cackling that Jacob did not love me and would leave me in the morning.

When the sun began to rise, Jacob awoke and touched my shoulder. My heart beat quickly as I turned my face. For a moment, Jacob appeared intrigued.

"Your eyes are clear, straight, and beautiful in the morning," he said dreamily.

Then he shot up with a startled cry. He yelled, "Where is Rachel? Where is my wife?"

"I am your wife," I whispered. "You spoke words of love to me last night."

I prayed silently to the God of Sarah and Abraham, Please let Jacob accept me.

Jacob cried out in rage, "I did not marry you. I labored for seven years to marry Rachel. I love her."

"Jacob, I am the sister who loves you, not Rachel," I said softly, looking down.

"You and your father have tricked me. You have robbed me of my rights," Jacob responded.

I wanted to run to Canaan, or Egypt. Instead, I fled our new house and ran back to my parents' house. I climbed the ladder to my old room, now Rachel's, alone. Behind me, I heard Jacob bellowing for my father in the courtyard. I found Rachel already awake, anxiously listening to Jacob's shouts. As soon as I saw Rachel, I began to cry uncontrollably. She was consoling me when we heard our father speak. He doomed our future with his words.

"Wait until the bridal week is over and you can marry Rachel also, provided you serve me another seven years," he said.

I unclasped Rachel's arms that were clutching my body and looked at my sister with puzzlement. She would marry my husband, the man I loved. I felt a gulf open between us. She could no longer be my friend or confidante. Rachel opened her mouth, but I spoke first.

"You are now my rival," I said.

I climbed down the ladder, ignoring her cries. I craved Jacob's love but knew that, for now, Rachel possessed it. When I reached the first floor, Jacob looked away and my father looked smug. My mother grabbed for my hand, but I avoided her grasp. With my head down in humiliation, I walked back across the courtyard to the house that I now shared with Jacob. Rachel would move into the four-room house by week's end, but for now, thankfully, it was my own refuge. My cousins Kishar and Zaltu watched me go by, and for once they had enough sense not to giggle.

I saw the truth. While Rachel and I had schemed with good intentions, my father had concealed his master plan. He knew Jacob wanted only Rachel. My father had tricked Jacob into seven more years of labor and married me off at the same time. I spent the bridal week secluded in the bedroom that I was meant to share with Jacob. I slept feverishly each night. Demons appeared in my dreams and tormented me by counting the days until Jacob married Rachel. Jacob did not visit me. My mother came to see me each morning, but I turned her away. Zilpah brought food and water and forced me to eat and drink. She said Jacob was seen wandering our valley during the day. On the sixth day, I heard my father and brothers move Rachel's belongings into the room next to mine. I pictured her identical bed and knew it would hold more joy than mine.

On Rachel's wedding day, Zilpah sat with me. Usually, her dull chatter annoyed me, but that day, I welcomed the distraction. Zilpah told me that my mother and Bilhah were taking Rachel to the river to bathe. Bilhah would serve as Rachel's attendant, in my absence. As the sun began to set, I told Zilpah to go to the wedding, for I did not want her to miss the festivities. In truth, I hoped that she might serve as my spy.

When I saw the lanterns flickering in the courtyard, I knew the wedding had begun. Laughter and song moved to a nearby wildflower field where the wedding canopy stood for the second week in a row. I tried to resist the temptation of watching the wedding. After losing this brief struggle with myself, I climbed to the roof where I could see the ceremony. As Rachel walked under the canopy, my father lifted her veil, and Jacob smiled with satisfaction. I saw Jacob mouth words to Rachel.

In unison with Rachel, I said, "And my beloved is mine."

I climbed down from the roof and went into Rachel's room. I fingered through her belongings. Concealed under a short pile of clothes, I found her *asherah* and the wide-eyed idol that Rafaela had given me years before. Rachel had to know that Jacob would forbid idols in his home. I broke the arms off my wide-eyed idol and, with silent pleasure, placed it and Rachel's *asherah* in the center of the bed.

Hours later, I heard Jacob and Rachel return to the house. Jacob laughed joyfully, but Rachel was silent. Suddenly, I heard Jacob yelp. I pictured him lying down on the idols, then jumping up, startled and bruised.

"In this house, we pray to the God of Sarah and Abraham," Jacob exclaimed. "Remove these idols. Bring them to your father's house or dispose of them. I do not care, but they will not remain here."

Rachel left the house without speaking. When she did not return, I heard Jacob pacing nervously. Good, I thought, he is worried that Rachel has abandoned him. I fell into a fitful sleep and dreamt of the night demon Lilith capturing my eyes. I pleaded with Lilith to reveal my sin.

"You ignored good sense and relied on trickery," Lilith shrieked as I slept.

I awoke trembling and reassured myself that Lilith did not exist. I heard Rachel preparing food for Jacob. I walked out of the room and saw her put blackberries and yogurt onto a plate.

"I believe that our husband prefers melon and cheese," I said curtly.

"Did you really need to break the arms off your idol?" Rachel responded. "I have so little of you left, my sister."

"You have my husband," I retorted, walking back into my room.

I dreaded seeing Rachel each morning, knowing that she held Jacob's heart. Thankfully, Rachel avoided our home as best as she could. Every morning, she awoke early to begin tending to the flock. She packed dried fruit on a string and cooked beans to eat when the sun reached its peak. In the evening, she returned after the other shepherds. Jacob grew restless at sundown, waiting for Rachel to return. Still, he shunned me. Each night, he followed Rachel into her room. I never heard any laughter coming from behind Rachel's door, only silence.

One morning, Jacob lingered in our home. I watched him loiter in the corner that I used as a workshop. He picked up and smelled the contents of different bottles. He held up a delicate blue bottle to a small window near the ceiling, letting the sun illuminate the bottle's murky contents. He sniffed its potion, which I knew smelled like strong leeks and garlic. He put down the bottle abruptly. I giggled.

"Why did you not warn me?" he said with mock anger.

The next morning after Rachel left to go to her flocks, Jacob lingered again. As I cleaned up our morning meal, he asked me if I was working on any new potions. I told him about my newest experiments with mandrakes. When Jacob left that morning, he put his hand on my shoulder.

"I have missed talking with you, Leah," he said.

Soon, Jacob and I fell into a routine. Rachel thought Jacob took his flocks to pasture shortly after she left. Instead, he stayed back and we spent time together. At night, Jacob slept with Rachel; during the day, he confided in me. I tried to be satisfied. Jacob asked if I still believed in the God of Sarah and Abraham. I assured him that I did.

"Leah, you and I are the guardians of God's message," he said.

Surprised at my own boldness, I said, "God promised Abraham and Sarah that they would have descendants as numerous as the sand by the sea and the stars in heaven. To preserve their legacy, Jacob, you and I must have children."

Jacob spent that night in my room.

Before we slept, he said, "You are my one true friend."

That night, I dreamt of angels leading me up a ladder to heaven. At the top of the ladder, Jacob appeared and embraced me.

In the morning, Rachel said, "You need not gloat. I enjoyed a night of peace and quiet."

I quickly devised a plan. If I could have children before Rachel, Jacob surely would grow to favor me. I began drinking my own mandrake potion, which until now I had only fed to sheep and goats. Each morning after Rachel and Jacob left, I swallowed a small cup of the bitter mixture. Although Jacob rarely visited me at night, I soon became pregnant. In quick succession, I had four sons. Each of my sons brought me joy for a different reason. Reuben, the eldest, devoted himself to caring for me and his younger brothers. Simeon and Levi made all of us laugh with their antics. Judah, who was the youngest, was also the most sensitive. Jacob loved his sons and honored me because of them.

Jacob, who used to prize Rachel, began to lose patience with her. He visited me more often at night. At first, I thought that Rachel's despair was my good luck. But Jacob talked only of Rachel. My wounds of rejection, which had begun to heal, opened up again.

"Rachel wants children so badly that she acts as if a childless life is worthless," Jacob said to me one night. "Am I not enough for her?'"

I could no longer hold my tongue.

"Am I not enough for you?" I said hotly. "I have given you love and sons. I believe in your God, unlike Rachel. Beauty is the only thing that I do not have to give."

Jacob put his arm around me and said, "I do love you, Leah. I just love Rachel differently."

In her desperation for a child, Rachel gave Bilhah to Jacob as a concubine. Bilhah giggled and grinned when Jacob asked her to join him for a night.

"Do you not think our husband has enough romance with two wives?" I asked Rachel sharply. "Does he also need Bilhah?'"

Bilhah soon gave birth to two sons. Fueled by my rivalry with Rachel, I gave Zilpah to Jacob. In time, she gave birth to twin sons, Gad and Asher, whom she smothered with love. Even though she never showed any affection for Jacob, Zilpah's sour face and tired eyes sparkled in her sons' presence. Caring for sons occupied nearly all of Zilpah's time. She rarely found time to search for herbs and plants for me anymore. I reminded her that she was my maidservant and responsible for chores. My reprimand did little good. Reuben witnessed my frustration and volunteered to collect mandrakes for me. I looked at my eldest son and realized that he was a young man, certainly strong enough to dig up mandrakes and collect other plants and herbs. One afternoon, I saw Rachel staring at Reuben as he returned with mandrake roots.

That evening, when Jacob was spending time with Bilhah, I heard a quiet knock on my bedroom door. I opened it to find Rachel on my threshold. She begged me for my mandrake potion. I refused. She promised me "a night of romance" with Jacob in return for the medicine. I refused again. Only when she spoke from the heart did I listen. She told me that, with four sons, I was the victor in our rivalry. She said that she envied me.

"I do not want a child for Jacob," Rachel said. "I just want to be a mother."

I took a long look at Rachel. She had lost the beauty of her youth. I had given Jacob more children than Rachel could ever hope to have. I reached for the mandrake potion. Rachel stood nervously as I poured it for her.

One moon passed, then six moons, then two years. My potion did not help Rachel. While I had two more sons, Issachar and Zebulan, Rachel remained barren. But Rachel never gave up hope. Whenever Rachel returned for more mandrake potion, I dutifully refilled her bottle. Over time, I grew to pity to Rachel, and I prayed for her.

I felt guilty when I told Rachel that I was pregnant once again. She just smiled and said nothing. After six sons, I finally bore a daughter. I named her Dinah. As I held Dinah for the first time, I called Rachel into the birthing room.

"I gave sons to Jacob. I want to share my daughter with you," I said, handing Dinah to her. "Will you help raise Dinah with me?"

"Thank you, sister," Rachel replied weeping. "I will treat Dinah as my own."

Before Dinah's first birthday, Rachel confided in me that her period of women had not come in two moons.

"Can I truly be pregnant?" Rachel asked. "If I let myself believe that I am pregnant, I worry that I will be disappointed."

On Rachel's slender body, her belly bulged early. She let herself trust that, soon, she would be a mother. After a long labor, she bore a son and named him Joseph.

As Rachel recovered from Joseph's difficult birth, Jacob and I made plans for our future. To fulfill the legacy of Abraham and Sarah, we wished to bring our family to Canaan. But we knew that my father would never willingly let us leave. Jacob and I would need to be shrewd in our planning and ask Rachel for her help. Together, Jacob, Rachel and I planned and prepared. One morning, after many months of preparation, we smuggled our children, our servants and handmaids, and our belongings out of our home. We stole away, leaving the village of Nahor behind forever.

In defiance and pride, I refused to walk out of Nahor with a veil hiding my face. No longer did I feel like a misfit. My sons and daughter surrounded me, as did my husband's wealth. My eyes might be weak, but my mind and body were strong. I was a wife, a mother, a sister, and a medicine woman. I had discovered my purpose.

Leah takes mandrake roots and places them in Lilith's ark. She gives the ark to her daughter, Dinah, when she becomes a young woman. She tells Dinah, "When life is difficult, open this ark and listen."

7 | DINAH: THE PAINTED JACKET

A HINT FROM TORAH:

Now Dinah, the daughter whom Leah had borne to Jacob, went out to visit the daughters of the land.

GENESIS 34:1

Dinah, whose name means "justice," is Leah and Jacob's only daughter. She grows up with 10 older brothers. Only Rachel's sons, Joseph and Benjamin, are born after her. Dinah is a young girl when her family escapes from her grandfather Laban and journeys to Canaan. Once in Canaan, the family settles near the city of Shechem. A chieftain named Hamor rules the region. Hamor's son is named Shechem after the city that his father controls. When Hamor enters Dinah's life, her story becomes one of violence and retribution. Sometimes terrible things can happen to people. This story is about a terrible thing that happened to Dinah. It is also about how she found the strength to recover.

Let us meet Dinah…

I have only faded memories of the village of Nahor, the place of my birth. I can picture my grandmother Adinah serving honey cakes and my grandfather Laban arguing with my father. In my mind's eye, I can conjure an image of a courtyard with a sycamore tree and children playing tag. I am not sure whether these images are my own or whether my mother and my auntie-mother, Rachel, talked about the village so often that their recollections became my memories. We fled Nahor during the sheep-shearing season after I turned five. Although my memories of Nahor are scattered, I remember every detail of our escape and desert adventure.

It began one morning a little past dawn. My mother ushered my brothers and me to the roof of our house.

"Come, let us watch your grandfather leave for the sheep-shearing festival in Haran," my mother said. "Although he does not know it, we will not see him again. I want to say good riddance. He deals only through trickery and greed."

From the roof, I watched my grandfather herding a small flock of white sheep away from our village. When he was safely out of view, my mother spat over the edge of the roof. I had never seen her spit before. In unison, my brothers and I spat as well. My mother went back inside to finish packing our belongings hastily.

Inside the house, I sat my younger half brother Joseph on my lap and, together, we watched the flurry of activity around us. My maidservant-mothers, Zilpah and Bilhah, prepared food for the journey. My brothers Reuben, Simeon, Levi, and Judah carried heavy items down from the second floor. Issachar and Zebulun chased one another around the house until they trampled over Joseph and me. Joseph began to cry. I got up and chased Issachar and Zebulun away.

"Enough," my mother yelled to my brothers and me. "I will leave you behind if you keep misbehaving."

My mother forbade us from telling anybody about our escape, not even our grandmother. I adored our grandmother, for she let me put on her jewelry and told me stories about growing up with my other grandmother, Rebekah.

"I want to say good-bye to Grandmother," I whimpered to my mother. "Please. Let me tell her that I will finally meet Grandmother Rebekah."

"If I allow you to tell your grandmother that we are leaving, your father will be angry with me," my mother told me. "Your grandmother will know that you meant to say good-bye."

When our belongings were packed, our father summoned us to the main room of the house.

"Today, we leave for our true home in the Promised Land," said our father. "For 20 years, I have dreamt of this moment, bringing my sons back to the land of my birth, the land promised by God to Abraham."

He had assembled our camels and flocks out of sight, hidden beyond a cluster of olive trees. In small groups, we quietly left our house to join him. Reuben, Simeon, and Levi sat on our rooftop, watching the village to make sure that our escape was not detected. Reuben came downstairs to signal that it was safe for my mother and me to leave. We held hands and walked out of our village for the last time. My mother held her head high, staring forward with a determined look on her face.

"Mama, you have forgotten your veil," I whispered, looking at her mismatched eyes.

"I know," she said firmly. "I will not leave Nahor covered up and hidden. I want to witness our departure."

It took nearly half a day to reassemble our family and our servants in the olive grove. Finally, my father lifted me onto a camel with Judah and told him to wrap his arms tightly around my waist.

"I can hold onto the camel myself," I responded. "I will not fall."

Our camel took her place in the caravan. My father rode the first camel, holding Joseph in front of him. Joseph sat tall, like a prince. My brothers and I knew that our father favored Joseph. I pretended not to care, but my brothers taunted Joseph at every opportunity. To make matters worse, from the moment that he could speak, Joseph provoked my brothers with predictions about the future. Joseph's predictions usually came to pass, further infuriating our brothers.

My mother walked clumsily next to our caravan of camels, now wearing a thick veil to protect her eyes. My father had prepared a camel for her to ride, but my mother insisted on putting the ingredients for her potions, ointments, and medicines on this camel rather than riding it herself. She directed the camel by pulling its reins from the ground as she walked.

Zilpah, sitting on a camel of her own, watched my mother struggle. She broke the silence of our escape to call out, "Leah, let my sons carry your supplies. Asher and Gad are walking empty-handed. Then you can ride your camel."

My mother pretended to ignore her, but grumbled, "I trust this camel more than your sons."

Before nightfall, we arrived at the bank of the Euphrates. As the sun began to set, we waded through the waters. My father, elder brothers, and Rachel made many trips over the river, bringing our animals and belongings to safety. I sat on the riverbank with Joseph. With the river separating us from my grandfather, we could talk and play once again.

On the far side of the river, we set up camp. In the moons leading up to our escape, Bilhah had secretly woven tent cloth out of camel hair, for it resisted rainwater. Then Zilpah dyed the cloth black. Simeon and Levi had never pitched a tent before, yet were entrusted with this duty. Joseph and I sat on the ground and watched with amusement as they struggled to pull the tent taut.

Joseph giggled, "That tent will fall."

A moment later, the tent collapsed. Simeon walked over and kicked sand at Joseph's face.

My mother, six brothers, and I shared a large tent. I felt grown up, sleeping next to Judah, Issachar, and Zebulun. In our village, I had shared a small annex room with only Joseph. All my other brothers slept in one large room that smelled like sweat. On our first night in the desert, we eavesdropped on Reuben talking with Bilhah in the night air. Reuben had just turned 14, while Bilhah was 21 and a mother. My mother said that Bilhah was a flirt.

Just as I drifted off to sleep, Issachar whispered that desert lions sometimes eat young girls. My other brothers laughed.

"Dinah is a little girl, boys," called my mother from the opposite side of the tent. "You will scare her with your tales."

"They do not scare me," I said.

Issachar responded by growling loudly and poking me in the back.

"If you disturb her one more time, you will sleep next to me," my mother said sternly.

That night, I closed my eyes and tried to sleep. With every sound I heard, I imagined prowling desert lions.

Each night, my brothers whispered about lions, scorpions, and wild boars.

Each morning, they practiced belching. I was not used to spending so much time with them. In our village, I had as many girl cousins as I had brothers. My cousins called me their sister, and whenever I tired of my 11 brothers, I escaped to their homes. In the desert, I was the only girl, unless I counted my mother, Rachel, Bilhah, and Zilpah.

I found refuge in Rachel and Joseph's tent. Rachel listened as I told her how I missed my grandmother. Then she swore me to secrecy and showed Joseph and me two idols that my grandmother had given her.

"Your father will destroy these idols if he finds them," Rachel said. "Your grandmother guessed that we would be leaving. She gave me these idols to help me remember her. I can share them with you."

"If Grandmother knew that we were leaving, I could have said good-bye," I said sadly.

"You can ask Grandfather to say good-bye to Grandmother when he visits us in the desert," Joseph suggested.

"We have escaped your grandfather and his greed. He will not be visiting us," Rachel replied quickly.

After a week in the desert, the village of Nahor became a distant memory until late one afternoon. Grandfather Laban barged into our camp with several of my uncles. Joseph and I were playing with the idols in Rachel's tent when we heard him yelling at our father. Joseph and I scurried onto Rachel's lap, huddling in her arms.

"I told you," Joseph said proudly.

Rachel whispered, "Let's be quiet. I want to hear what your grandfather says."

Grandfather Laban shouted, "Why did you flee in secrecy and mislead me? You did not even let me kiss my grandchildren and daughters good-bye! And why did you steal my idols?"

Rachel tensed up when Grandfather Laban mentioned the idols.

"We left in secret because I was afraid that you would force Rachel and Leah to stay," my father said. "The idols are a different matter. I did not steal your idols. If anybody in my camp has taken them, that person shall not stay alive."

Rachel gasped. Joseph and I buried our faces against her.

Then she whispered to us, "Everything will be all right, children. I have a plan. Go out and greet your grandfather, but do not say a word about the idols."

As we left the tent, Rachel grabbed the idols and put them under the cushion on which she sat. Joseph and I followed behind Grandfather Laban as he inspected Bilhah's tent, then Zilpah's tent, then my mother's tent, and finally Rachel's tent.

"Please excuse my rudeness, Father, for I cannot stand up to greet you. I have my period of women," said Rachel, holding her stomach and grimacing.

Grandfather Laban looked awkwardly at Rachel. He picked up the belongings around her and found nothing. When he left the tent, Joseph and I raced over to Rachel and hugged her.

"Do you believe in curses, Mama?" asked Joseph, with fear in his voice.

"No, of course not, my boy," Rachel answered, yet she sounded unsure.

The next morning, my father woke us just after dawn.

Speaking to my mother, he said, "Your father wants to kiss you and his grandchildren good-bye. Come quickly, and we will be rid of him."

I cringed when my grandfather leaned down to hug me.

"A girl should learn to give a better hug than that," my grandfather said.

I raced back and held my mother's hand. Together, we watched my grandfather turn to go home.

Around the campfire that evening, we all rejoiced. I had never seen my father so jovial. He laughed as my brothers chased one another. Simeon and Levi began to wrestle. My father watched them pin one another, making suggestions for their technique. I stood up and chased Joseph in circles. My father came over and picked me up high into the sky.

"How is my pretty girl?" he asked, putting me down next to my mother. "Joseph, why do you not chase your big brothers?"

My father remained cheerful and lighthearted as we traveled through the hill country. Then one day, we saw a river in the distance. My father walked up a steep hill to get a better view. When he returned, my brothers challenged him to wrestle. Just the previous day, my father had spent hours lifting my brothers over his head and pinning them on their backs.

"Not this afternoon, my sons," said my father, clenching his jaw.

My father pulled my mother and Rachel aside. They began to whisper. I ran up to my mother to hear their conversation, but she shooed me away. After they finished talking, my father gathered my brothers and me.

"This hill country is called Gilead. It is rich with fruit and vegetables to eat," he said. "We will rest here on the banks of the River Jabbok for one moon to allow the sheep, goats, and cattle to pasture in the fields and the camels to drink their fill from the river."

My brothers and I looked curiously at one another. Until now, my father had spoken only of traveling to Canaan as quickly as possible.

"We will not need to break down tents or set them up again for a full moon?" Simeon asked, beginning to smile.

"Enjoy yourselves," answered my father. "You have worked hard, sons. For now, you should rest. We still have quite a journey in front of us."

My mother asked Judah to watch over me so she could unpack her workshop. Judah and I went to explore the hills around us. We climbed the steepest hill, the one that our father had used as a lookout earlier in the day. From the top of the hill, we could see a small valley below. Not far from us, we spied our father talking with two servants. Camels packed for travel grazed nearby. Judah and I hid behind a bramble bush and listened.

Pacing, our father said, "Give him the following message: To my lord Esau, thus says your servant Jacob. I stayed with Laban until now. I have many cattle, donkeys, sheep, and servants. My lord, I hope to gain your favor."

My father never called anybody "lord" except God. The servants mounted the camels and rode off toward the river. His head down, my father walked toward our camp.

"Who is Esau?" I asked Judah.

"Our father's brother, our uncle, not a good man," said Judah. "He once threatened our father's life."

"Does Esau still want to kill our father?" I asked.

"I do not know," answered Judah

That night, as I tried to sleep, I kept imagining Esau capturing my whole family and making us servants. I sat up and saw my mother mixing lotions by the light of an oil lamp. I tiptoed over to her.

"Your bedtime has long passed, Dinah," my mother said. "Are you having trouble sleeping?"

"Judah and I overheard our father sending servants to find an uncle named Esau," I said fearfully. "Judah said that Esau once wanted to kill our father."

"You should not eavesdrop on your father," my mother said sternly. "You need not worry, though. Many, many years ago, your father and Esau fought, just like your brothers sometimes argue with one another. Your father feared Esau and ran away to our village. I trust that Esau forgave your father a long time ago."

For the next moon, I tried not to think about Esau. I trailed behind my brothers each morning as they picked fruit, tended to the sheep, and brought the camels to water. When I grew bored, I helped my mother mix lotions or played tag with Joseph. Each afternoon, I watched my brothers wrestle in the desert sand.

"Show me how to wrestle," I pleaded.

"Do not be foolish," Simeon answered. "You are a girl."

"Go get Joseph, and we will flip him on his back," Levi said. My brothers laughed.

"I want to learn to wrestle. Please show me how," I repeated.

Judah came over to me and said quietly, "Our brothers can get rough. You could get hurt. Besides, it is not proper for you to wrestle with us."

I stood up and stomped away toward our camp. As I walked through a pasture, I passed a small lamb. I began stroking the lamb, then reached under its belly. I pushed the lamb and tried to flip it onto its back. The lamb fell onto its side, and I crashed on top of it. Rachel came running.

"Dinah, did you hurt yourself?" she asked. "What are you doing?"

"My brothers like to wrestle but will not let me join them," I said. "I wanted to flip a sheep like you do when you shear their fleece. If I learn how, maybe my brothers will let me wrestle with them."

"Shearing a sheep requires skill. You cannot just push the animal on its side, or you and the sheep will get hurt," said Rachel. "Would you like me to teach you how to shear a sheep?"

First thing the next morning, I ran down to the pasture to find Rachel. Rachel took a small spotted ewe from the flock and drove it to a creek. She rinsed the dust, grime, and dung from the ewe's coat. She lifted the ewe up on her two hind hooves and, with copper scissors, clipped off dirty ends from the fleece on the ewe's underside.

"First remove the dirty patches. You must work quickly or you will scare the sheep," Rachel said, resting the ewe on all four hooves again. "Talk to her as you clip to calm her nerves."

Rachel put her arm under the ewe and, in one swift move, flipped the

animal over onto its back. Rachel held the ewe's hind legs, quickly but carefully clipping fleece off her chest and neck. Then Rachel released the ewe's legs
and the animal struggled back up onto her hooves. Rachel clipped fleece off
the ewe's back.

Then she chose a small lamb from the flock. She showed me how to turn
the lamb painlessly onto his back. I practiced wrestling the lamb until Rachel
told me to let the poor animal rest. That night, I told my mother and brothers
how Rachel had taught me to pin a lamb. My mother smiled, but my brothers
told me that a girl could wrestle only the smallest of animals.

"Soon, I will be able to wrestle you," I persisted.

"Brothers protect their sisters. They do not fight them," Levi responded.

My brothers' remarks only made me more determined. Each day, I went
to Rachel and she coached me in shearing sheep. I almost forgot about Esau and
the servants. One afternoon in the pasture, I looked up and saw camels gallop-
ing toward our camp. The servants stopped in front of Rachel. "Where is Jacob?"
they called out. "We have word from Esau. He is approaching with 400 men."

Rachel jumped onto one of the camels, holding the servant around his
waist.

"Dinah, tell your mother to meet your father and me at his tent," Rachel
instructed. Turning to the servants, she said, "Jacob has taken a flock to pasture.
We must find him."

I ran back to camp and found my mother cold-pressing desert flowers.

"How is my little shepherdess?" she asked smiling.

"The servants have come back. Uncle Esau is coming with 400 men," I
cried. "Rachel says to meet her and Father in his tent."

My mother rushed out. The news spread quickly through camp, and my
brothers came back to our tent to wait with me. Near dinnertime, our mother
returned.

"Your father wants us to divide into two camps. We will stay here with
Zilpah, Gad, and Asher. Rachel and Bilhah and their boys are leaving tonight.
They will camp beyond that steep hill. Your father will stand guard on the hill
with the servants," my mother said. "If Esau comes to one camp, then the other
camp will escape."

I hurried outside to say good-bye to Rachel and Joseph. My father knelt
nearby, looking up at the heavens. I shuddered when I saw him.

"Deliver me, I pray, from the hand of my brother, from the hand of Esau," pleaded my father. "I fear he may come and strike my family down, mothers and children alike."

The next morning, my father took nearly half our flock. He instructed the servants to bring these animals to Esau as gifts.

Divided into two camps, we moved toward the River Jabbok. By nightfall, we reached its steep banks, and our camps joined back together. The currents of the Jabbok flowed powerfully and swiftly. When Simeon and Levi waded into the river, they struggled not to be swept away. Reuben told me to climb onto his shoulders. He carried me across and returned to carry Bilhah and, then, our mother. I watched Rachel struggle to carry a large ewe across the water. In the center of the river, the water pulled her underneath, and she disappeared. The ewe fell out of her arms and was lost in the currents. I could not see Rachel. I thought of the idols and my father's curse. I screamed.

Standing next to me, Joseph said clearly, "My mother will be all right."

A moment later, Rachel emerged coughing and gasping for breath. Our father jumped into the river and pulled her to shore. Joseph and I ran over to embrace her. Leah wrapped a blanket around Rachel's shoulders.

After our whole camp made it across the river, Bilhah and Zilpah cooked lentil stew over the fire. We ate it quickly, for we were cold and hungry. Our father stood by the campfire, staring back across the Jabbok.

"I must return to the other side of the River Jabbok," my father finally said. "God calls me back to the opposite bank."

My whole family stared at my father. My stomach turned in knots.

"Jacob, you brought your wives, sons, and daughter to this side of the Jabbok," responded my mother, breaking the silence. "Now, will you leave us to fend for ourselves? Think of your children."

I had never heard my mother talk back to my father. Rachel walked over and stood next to my mother, joined by Bilhah and Zilpah.

"Do you believe so completely in your God that you would abandon us here?" asked Rachel.

"I must pray and prepare myself to meet Esau," our father replied. "I promise to return to you at dawn."

My father turned and dove into the river. We watched him swim until he disappeared into the darkness of night. My mother turned to my brothers and me.

"Your father simply needs to think. We will be safe here," she said, as though we had not heard her argue with him.

Simeon and Levi raised only one tent. My 11 brothers and I crowded into this tent, our mats touching each other. My mother, Rachel, Bilhah, and Zilpah joined the servants to sit guard outside the tent by the light of the campfire.

We were silent until Simeon whispered that he felt certain that he could tackle Esau single-handedly.

"Esau has 400 men with him," Judah replied. "You will tackle all of them?"

Ignoring my brothers, Reuben said, "I am going outside to sit with Bilhah and our mother. The women should not be left to guard with only servants to help them."

Shortly after Reuben left, I drifted off to sleep with Joseph in my arms. At dawn, I heard my mother shout and Rachel cry. My brothers and I rushed outside. Our father staggered up from the riverbed, his clothes tattered and his face covered with scratches. He limped, his left leg trailing behind him.

"A desert lion attacked him," cried out Issachar.

"Be quiet," called my mother, racing to my father's side with Rachel.

My father rested one arm around my mother's shoulder and the other arm around Rachel's shoulder. Together, they shuffled toward us.

"I wrestled with an angel of God," my father said in a weak, hoarse voice. "When I prevailed, the angel blessed me and changed my name to Israel."

Rachel looked at my mother and rolled her eyes in doubt.

"Jacob, come to the tent," my mother said. "I will put a cool salve on your cuts."

My brothers and I followed them back to the tent, but we waited outside as they entered. My brothers calmed their nerves by wrestling. They cheered the champion of each match by calling him "Israel." Only Reuben sat off in the distance, staring toward the horizon.

At midday, Reuben yelled out, "Beware! Men are approaching on camels."

My father heard Reuben's warning and limped out of the tent as quickly as he could. Peering into the distance, my father said, "It is Esau."

Then he spoke to my brothers. "My sons, each of you stand by your own mother."

I looked around awkwardly until my mother waved me over next to her. Nervously, we huddled together and watched in silence as Esau approached. I bit into my lip when Esau was close enough for me to see his red hair and ruddy skin. Esau focused his eyes on my father. He dismounted his camel. Several of his men rode up next to him, but remained high above us on their camels.

My father limped toward his brother, bowing seven times as he moved forward. I had never seen my father bow to another person. I felt embarrassed for him and fearful. Esau ran forward. We all gasped, and Bilhah began to cry. Esau threw his arms around my father's neck. Reuben and Judah raced to protect our father, not knowing what Esau intended. Esau kissed my father on both cheeks, smiled, and then wept.

My father laughed and wiped tears from his own eyes.

Esau noticed us and asked, "Who are these with you?"

"God has blessed me with many children," my father answered, waving to Zilpah and Bilhah. Zilpah and Bilhah brought forward Gad, Asher, Dan, and Naphtali.

"Bow to your Uncle Esau, my sons," my father urged. "Show him respect."

My mother walked out next, linking arms with my six brothers and me. When she stood before Esau, my mother raised her veil and looked straight at him. When Esau did not flinch at the sight of her eyes, my mother smiled and bowed.

Finally, Rachel approached Esau, holding Joseph's hand. She lifted Joseph into her arms and bowed. Esau put his arm around my father and said, "You have done well, my brother."

My father invited Esau into our tent, and they entered alone. All afternoon, we heard them talking and laughing.

"Why does Father call Esau 'my lord'?" I asked my mother as we prepared food.

"Your father wants to show respect to Esau," she answered.

"My father has always said that God is our only Lord," I said in protest.

After the feast, Esau left to return home. My father promised that we would follow him. The next morning, though, we awoke and began journeying in the opposite direction.

"Why did Father break his promise to Esau?" I asked my mother.

"Your father made peace with Uncle Esau," said my mother. "But Esau is part of your father's past, not his future."

Our family journeyed to the village Succoth. My father built a house for our family and stalls for our animals. To celebrate our home's completion, my mother and Rachel prepared to host my grandmother Rebekah at the new moon. Rachel selected the choicest lambs for the meal. My mother mixed sweet-smelling perfumes and lotions to give to Rebekah as gifts. My mother and I went to a small oasis to bathe. She gave me a new tunic to wear.

Grandmother Rebekah arrived on a camel, sitting tall on a saddle decorated with jewels. She had silver hair that sparkled in the sun, and she wore flowing white robes. Her face looked young, yet wise and serene. A white-haired maidservant named Deborah accompanied her. My father raced to help her from the camel. He introduced Rachel, then my mother, and finally Zilpah and Bilhah. He proudly lined up my brothers and told them to bow.

Rebekah nodded and said, "I hear that you have been blessed with a daughter."

Smiling widely, I walked forward.

"I am Dinah," I said shyly. "My Grandmother Adinah spoke kind words about you."

"Adinah was my dearest friend. I still miss her, after all these years. The God of Sarah and Abraham has blessed you, my son," said Grandmother Rebekah, looking straight at me. "I feel blessed as well."

She put her arms around my mother and Rachel. "We have much to talk about, my daughters," she said. "Show me to your tent, and we will learn about one another."

I trailed behind Grandmother Rebekah, my mother, and Rachel.

As they entered Rachel's tent, my mother turned to me and said, "Not now, Dinah. You will see your grandmother later. Go find Bilhah and Zilpah and help them with the feast or play with your brothers."

Disappointed, I went to find my brothers. As usual, they were wrestling in the sand.

"Grandmother Rebekah seemed to like you," Simeon said jealously.

"I suppose," I responded, sitting down to watch.

"Stand up, and I will show you some wrestling moves," Levi said.

Eagerly, I ran over to him. All morning, Levi and Simeon showed me how to flip and pin an opponent. By the time our feast began, my tunic was torn, my hair disheveled, and my face covered with dust.

"What have you done to yourself?!" asked my mother.

"My brothers taught me to wrestle," I said proudly.

"Girls do not wrestle," said Deborah critically.

Embarrassed, I struggled to hold back my tears.

"After the feast, Dinah, we will sit and talk," said Grandmother Rebekah. "I want to get to know you, my child. We can talk about what is appropriate for a young woman."

Throughout the feast, I worried that I had offended Grandmother Rebekah. Perhaps she would not accept me as a granddaughter or, even worse, blame my mother for my boorish behavior. My mother would not forgive me if Grandmother Rebekah favored Rachel over her.

Nervously, I sought out Grandmother Rebekah after the feast. In a kind voice, she told me about the God of Sarah and Abraham and talked about the responsibility of their legacy.

"You are a daughter of Sarah, chosen by God. We behave in a certain manner," she said. "I, too, was a shepherd girl. You may still herd the flocks and shear the animals, but you must do so with dignity."

We stayed in Succoth through six sheep-shearing seasons. Grandmother Rebekah visited nearly each new moon. My breasts grew round and my periods of women began. I befriended a girl named Alit, the daughter of a man named Shua. Alit and I became nearly inseparable.

Once, when Alit came to visit, I showed her how Rachel had taught me to shear a sheep. One after another, I lifted lambs and ewes and pinned them onto their backs. Alit laughed at me.

"You look like a boy, wrestling with those sheep," she said with a giggle. Suddenly, I noticed my father approaching.

"I agree with Alit," he said. "You do look like an unruly boy, even though you are a young woman." A few days later, my father brought me a present, a jacket made of the purest white silk.

"You are growing older, Dinah," he said. "I have bought you this jacket so you will present yourself as a maiden destined to marry well."

I put on the jacket. It felt smooth, cool, and luxurious but awkward on my body. I was accustomed to wearing clothes that I could dirty. I asked Zilpah for the dyes that she used on yarn. I painted the jacket with bright colors, decorating it with scenes of the village of Nahor, the Euphrates River, the hill country of Gilead, and the River Jabbok.

I was nervous when I showed the jacket to Alit. To my surprise, she liked it. My mother and Rachel also said the jacket was beautiful. My father, however, was furious.

"I purchased that jacket to provide you with the clothes of a fine, young woman," my father said sternly. "Peasants and poor shepherdesses wear crudely painted clothing, not the daughters of chieftains."

"Many people wear even more colorful clothing," I said.

"Stop arguing. You are not 'many people,' Dinah. You are my daughter. You must stop behaving like a simple shepherd girl and begin to envision yourself as a young maiden, part of our family's legacy. Besides, look at the pictures that you painted. We no longer live in Nahor and we left the Euphrates and Jabbok far behind us. You need not wear such a reminder," said my father.

I considered appealing to my mother but knew that she would never confront my father over something as trivial as a jacket. So I hid the jacket under my bed and told my father that I had given it away. Whenever I went to visit Alit, I hid the jacket in my bag and put it on when I could not longer see my family's home.

At the end of the sixth sheep-shearing season, my father decided to move our family from Succoth in search of better pastures. Grandmother Rebekah had told him about fertile grazing land near the city of Shechem. He took Reuben, Simeon, and Levi to explore Shechem and the pastures surrounding it. When they returned home, my father already had purchased a plot of land on which to build our home. I did not want to leave Alit, but my mother promised that I could visit. Our new house was just over the Jordan River from Succoth. Soon, I would be old enough to visit her on my own.

As soon as we arrived in Shechem, my father invited the chieftain of the land, a man named Hamor, to a feast. My father had purchased our land from this man and wanted to impress him with our family. Hamor arrived with a son just a few years older than me.

"My name is Shechem, like the city," said his son, bowing in front of my father. He looked at me and smiled.

"That handsome boy likes you," whispered Bilhah.

"Do you think so?" I giggled.

Soon, Shechem visited my brothers nearly every day. He would wrestle with Simeon, Levi, and Judah. When they took a break, Shechem would sit next to me and make jokes. I laughed at his jokes, even the ones that were not funny.

One day, Joseph saw me sitting with Shechem and came over to talk.

Shechem said, "Leave us alone." My brothers laughed as Joseph walked away.

When my brothers were not listening, I said quietly, "Shechem, I spend a lot of time with Joseph."

Shechem replied, "I know he is your brother. But why do you like that runt?"

The next time that Shechem came to our camp to wrestle, I avoided him. I sat down next to Reuben to watch my brothers play.

"Dinah, didn't you see me sitting right over there?" Shechem said, coming over and sitting on the ground next to me.

When nobody was looking, he took some of my hair and started twirling it in his fingers. I did not like his hand in my hair and bent my head away from him to free it.

When Shechem got up to wrestle Judah, Reuben leaned over to me and said, "Our father and I are pleased to see that you and Shechem are getting along. His family is wealthy and influential. They have a grand palace in the city."

Shechem pinned Judah to the ground. He stood up, lifted his arms to the sky, and looked toward me.

"Did you see me pin your weakling brother, Dinah?" he said, sitting down next to me. "I see that Joseph's mother is pregnant again. I guess Joseph will not be the runt anymore."

I started to leave, but Shechem held onto my arm tightly. I said softly, "Shechem, please stop pulling at my arm. It hurts."

Shechem let go and said smugly, "I will see you soon, Dinah."

When I got back to my tent, I looked at my arm. It was blue and purple where Shechem had clutched it. I did not know what to do. I thought about telling my mother, but she was absorbed with Rachel and her difficult pregnancy.

I considered talking to Reuben or Judah, but they were Shechem's friends. I confided in Joseph. He listened to my story and looked at the bruise.

"You jest that I predict the future. Listen to me, and this time do not laugh. Shechem will try to hurt you again," Joseph said. "You need to avoid him."

"How can I?" I replied. "He visits our brothers nearly every day."

Joseph's premonition frightened me. Thankfully, it would be several days before I saw Shechem again. I had plans to visit Alit and attend a party thrown by her cousin, a girl slightly younger than us. I could talk to Alit about Shechem.

My family was camped on the top of a hill. To travel to visit Alit, I rode my camel down into the valley. Looking up over my shoulder, I saw our camp and the foundation of the house that the servants were building for us. When I could not see the camp anymore, I dismounted the camel and took my colorful jacket out of my bag. Just then, Shechem appeared from behind a tree.

"Why are you here?" I asked.

"I heard you tell Simeon that you planned to visit a friend," Shechem said grinning. "I thought we could get to know one another better, alone."

Before I knew what was happening, Shechem put his hands on my shoulders and began kissing me. He pushed his face into mine with force. I struggled to breathe and pulled away.

"Stop," I gasped. "What are you doing?"

"Nobody will see us here," Shechem said, pulling me toward him again.

I tried to knock Shechem down, putting my arm around his stomach as though I were flipping a sheep. Shechem was too heavy and strong. He pinned me in the dirt. I tried to scream, "No, stop, rape!" I could not find the words.

I kicked and punched at Shechem and held down my tunic. Shechem tore my tunic open, pushing his body into my nakedness.

I wailed loudly but nobody heard.

After Shechem was finished, he tried to hold me. I recoiled.

"I love you, Dinah," Shechem said. "You will be my wife and live in my family's fortress."

I stood up, grabbed my jacket, and ran to my camel.

"Where are you going?" Shechem asked. "Do you plan to go home with a torn tunic and dirt in your hair? Your father will know immediately that you allowed me to be intimate with you. He will call you immodest. Come with me to my home, and I will treat you as my bride."

I hoisted myself painfully onto my camel. Shechem ran toward me and pulled me off. I screamed and kicked. He tossed me onto his own camel and lifted himself onto the animal behind me. Holding me tightly around the waist, he whipped the camel into gallop. I clawed at Shechem's hands. As we approached his family's fortress, Shechem told me to be modest and cover myself up. I put on my jacket over my torn clothing. The bright colors no longer fit me. I wished the jacket could be white and pure again.

Shechem brought me through a back entrance of his family's fortress. I resisted entering, but he pushed me through the door and into a long hallway. Rich tapestries covered the floors, and oil lamps lit our way. Shechem pulled me by the wrist up a stone staircase. He brought me to a room with a large wooden bed in the center. A bright crimson and purple blanket covered the bed. I cringed, imagining Shechem throwing me on the bed and tearing my clothes from my body. But he did not enter the room.

"Clean yourself up," Shechem said. "I will send a maidservant to draw water for you. I will ask her to bring you sweet-smelling perfume and clothes meant for a bride. Meanwhile, I will speak to my father and tell him that I have acquired you as my wife. Tonight, we will have romance."

When Shechem left, he locked the door. I picked up a stool and carried it to the only window, which was small and near the ceiling. By standing on the stool, I could see outside. In the distance, I saw my family's camp. I thought of my mother and Rachel and began to cry. Just then, I heard Shechem arguing with his father in the hallway.

"What have you done? You cannot just capture that girl and make her your wife," Hamor said to his son. "The girl's father is a religious man, a friend, and a chieftain in his own right. Besides, he has many sons and servants. We do not wish to insult and anger him."

"You are the chieftain of this entire land, and I am your son," Shechem said. "Certainly, I can acquire the daughter of a lowly shepherd on my own. She should be pleased with her new wealth."

"Shechem, you have acted impulsively," Hamor answered. "We must go at once and ask Jacob for his daughter. If we do not, he and his sons will cause trouble. I guarantee it."

Shechem's and Hamor's voices faded away as they walked down the hallway. I heard the key turn in the lock. An elderly maidservant stood in the doorway carrying a basin and a jar of water. She looked sadly at my torn clothing, but said nothing.

"My master Shechem asked me to bring water, soap, and perfume to you," she said quietly, looking down.

"Do you know when Shechem will return?" I asked, trembling.

"My masters Shechem and Hamor have left the palace to speak with your father," she answered. "I have brought a silk tunic and a light meal of wine, grapes, and cheese."

"What is your name?" I asked, sensing kindness in the old woman's voice.

"I am Hebat," she responded, putting her hand on my arm. She touched a bruise, and I winced. "My husband, Moti, is caretaker of the palace, and I am caretaker of the family."

I undressed slowly and poured water over my body. The water's coolness reminded me of crossing the Euphrates and the River Jabbok. Hebat dried me off and helped me into an indigo silk tunic meant for a wealthy woman to wear to bed. I ate a few pieces of cheese and some grapes as Hebat tidied up the room.

"My master Shechem will return shortly," Hebat said. "May I help you with your makeup or your hair?"

"Thank you for your kindness," I replied. "I can apply my makeup and do my hair myself."

Hebat left again, locking the door behind her. I stood on the stool and looked out the window. In the distance, I saw Shechem, Hamor, and several servants returning to the fortress. I shuddered. I climbed into the bed and began to weep. Hours passed, and darkness descended outside. Shechem did not return. I drifted off into a fitful sleep, waking often in fear.

In the morning, I heard men screaming in pain. Hebat returned, bringing yogurt, bread, and pomegranates.

"My master Shechem must love you very much," she said. "To marry you, he demanded that all the men of the city be circumcised. He has already taken a knife to himself and retreated to his bedroom in pain."

"All of the men?" I asked in disbelief.

Silently, I relished the image of Shechem doubled over in pain.

"You will remain here while Shechem recovers," Hebat said. "I will care for you and also look after my husband. He has injured himself like the other men."

For two days, I saw only Hebat. She brought me food in the morning, at midday, and in the evening. We spoke very little. Whenever Hebat left, she locked the door and I stood on the stool and looked out the window. I wondered whether my mother had pleaded with my father on my behalf. I wondered whether Rachel knew that I had fought back. I prayed that Shechem's wound might become infected and he would die.

On my third day in the fortress, I awoke to the sounds of screams and wails throughout the city. I rushed to look out the window. I saw a guard lying dead below me. The sounds of battle and bloodshed filled the air. I sat on the edge of my bed and waited in fear.

Finally, Hebat opened the door. Her eyes were red and swollen. I heard familiar voices. Simeon and Levi pushed Hebat into the room. Blood covered my brothers' hands and dripped from their sandals. Each carried a sword.

"Your brothers have killed my Moti and all the men of the city," Hebat cried, tearing her clothes in grief. "Shechem is dead. It is your fault."

She spat at my feet. Simeon walked in front of Hebat.

"Dinah, come with us," he said.

I looked back at Hebat but knew that I could not console her. As we walked through the fortress, I saw bloodied corpses on tapestry rugs. Women cried next to their fallen men, looking up with hateful, grief-stricken faces as we passed.

"Why?" I said to Simeon and Levi.

"Should our sister be treated as a whore?" Levi replied. "Shechem offended not only you but our family."

"Cover yourself," Simeon said, "A daughter of Israel should not dress so immodestly." I realized that I was wearing only a blue silk night tunic. I put on my painted jacket.

Outside the fortress, I stared at the corpses surrounding me. Simeon and Levi took my arms and ledme toward the fortress's sheep pens.

"You stay here until we return," Simeon said. "Levi and I will search the city for men in hiding. Back at our camp, we will contend with you."

Fear of my brothers and disgust at their rage filled my heart. When Simeon and Levi were out of view, I ran back toward the fortress. I found Shechem's camel still tied up outside the back entrance. Mounting it, I directed the camel toward my family's camp, then changed my mind. I turned toward Alit's house instead.

When I arrived at Alit's home, she was outside alone. She gasped when she saw my bruised face and torn jacket. She helped me from the camel. I told her what Shechem had done and how my brothers had avenged the attack.

"May I stay here?" I asked. "I do not want to talk to my mother or see my father just yet. I fear Simeon and Levi, for they are ruthless and full of rage. If they think that I allowed Shechem to have his way with me, they will harm me."

"Yes, my sister, of course," she said tenderly. "Your mother will worry, though. Let me send my friend Hirah the Adullamite to tell her that you found refuge at my house. Hirah is trustworthy."

When Hirah returned, Judah came with him, carrying a bag that our mother had packed with my belongings.

"Our father is concerned for our family's safety," Judah said. "We must leave Shechem. For now, we will stay at Grandmother Rebekah's home in Bethel. Our mother and I fear for you. Simeon and Levi are still fueled by fury. Your disappearance angered them even more."

"Dinah may stay here," said Shua, Alit's father. "Nobody knows she is here besides Hirah and us. We will watch over her, and she will be safe."

Judah embraced me and thanked Shua. He raced off to help move my family.

At Alit's home, I began to recover. Her mother and father treated me as their own daughter. Alit and I took long walks each day, and she held me when I cried. Nearly two moons passed, and I heard nothing of my family. My period of women did not come, and my waist grew larger. I tried to ignore my body's changes, but in my heart, I knew that I would have Shechem's baby. I told nobody, not even Alit. One evening, when Alit and I returned from picking olives for her mother, Judah sat outside her house.

"Tragedy has struck our family again," he said. "Our beloved auntie-mother Rachel died from childbirth. She only held her son Benjamin for a moment."

I fell down and began to cry. I thought of the idols that Rachel had hidden from my father and grandfather so many years ago. I had all but forgotten my father's impulsive curse. Now it had been fulfilled. My sorrow mixed with fear. Rachel died bearing a child. I felt my own belly.

"Judah, I am pregnant," I blurted out.

Judah stiffened and said, "You must leave Canaan. The child will share Shechem's blood. If you give birth to a boy, Simeon and Levi will track you down and kill the child."

Shua took Judah to find Hirah the Adullamite. He had grown up in a southern Canaanite town called Timnah. His family were traders who traveled to Timnah and Egypt often. Hirah knew of a caravan going to Egypt the next week. Judah paid the traders, and they allowed me to join them.

"Please tell our mother what has become of me," I said to Judah as I hugged him.

"I pray that we will meet someday again," he responded.

Judah helped me onto a camel. Alit and her parents waved good-bye. The caravan traveled through the Negev desert. I spoke to nobody until we reached the Red Sea. When I smelled the fresh ocean breeze, I mourned leaving my family and my ancestors' legacy, but I also felt free and safe. I touched my belly and prayed that my child would only know peace.

Dinah takes her jacket and places it in Lilith's ark. She gives the ark to her friend Alit before she leaves Canaan. Dinah says to Alit, "Please tell the girls after me to be survivors, not victims."

Alit safeguards the ark and gives it to her daughter-in-law Tamar.

8 | TAMAR: THE COPPER MIRROR

A HINT FROM TORAH:

So she took off her widow's garb, covered her face with a veil, and, wrapping herself up, sat down at the entrance to Enaim.... GENESIS 38:14

Tamar, whose name means "date palm," is born a Canaanite. Her story centers around an ancient Israelite tradition: when a man dies before his wife bears a son, the deceased's brother is obliged to marry his widow. Any children born from this second marriage are considered the offspring of the deceased. Tamar enters the biblical story when she marries Er, Judah's eldest son. But Er dies before Tamar bears a child. Tamar is obliged to marry Er's brother Onan. Soon after, Onan also dies. Judah sends Tamar away until his youngest son, Shelah, grows up. Years pass, and Judah does not send for Tamar. She is faced with the prospect of spending her life as a childless widow. Women in Tamar's time had limited control over their lives. She makes a painful choice to compromise herself in order to improve her life.

Let us meet Tamar...

My mother cradled my chin upward in her palm and delicately painted my eyelids with green malachite, wiping off the excess with her thumb. Dipping a small stick into black kohl, she outlined my eyes, extending the color in thin stripes on each side of my face. I tried not to fidget.

"Look straight ahead, Tamar," she directed as she knelt down and began painting my lips with a mixture of red ochre clay and gum resin. "Do not lick your lips."

When my mother finished with my makeup, I tied papyrus sandals onto my feet and tugged a white linen tunic over my head. The tunic fit tightly across my chest.

"I will need to sew you a new tunic soon enough. You are becoming a woman and this child's outfit does not flatter your new curves," my mother said, embracing me. I rolled my eyes and grimaced.

"Do not make faces," she said, pursing her lips. "Now that you have turned 14, can I no longer comment on your appearance or even give you a hug?

She positioned a black straight wig over my brown curly hair, then clasped a heavy, beaded collar around my neck. She stood back to admire her handiwork and lifted a polished copper mirror in front of my face. I saw an Egyptian princess staring back, rather than a Canaanite girl. I hardly recognized myself. I smiled broadly. Just then, my father walked into the room and looked at me.

"You have outdone yourself," he said, kissing my mother on the head. "Tamar's costume will dazzle the audience here in Timnah today, and so will your costume. When townsfolk and shepherds watch your performance, the stories of the gods will come alive for them."

My mother was dressed as the war goddess Anat. Watching her performance both delighted and frightened me. All of my mother's gentleness disappeared, and only intensity possessed her when she took the stage as Anat. The spirited actress that I witnessed hardly resembled the mother who badgered me about my looks and manners. Without speaking, she portrayed my father's characters solely through her facial expressions and body movements. I wanted to know such passion some day. Although my father was a master storyteller, crowds gathered not to listen to him but to watch my mother's chilling pantomimes.

My father was born into a family of storytellers. His father and grandfather had also traveled throughout Canaan, sharing the legends of gods, villains, queens, and kings. His father, my Grandpa Nabu, still traveled with us.

"We are keepers of the tales. Without us, the legends would be lost," Grandpa Nabu had told me. "It is a holy duty."

My mother had grown up the daughter of a goldsmith, a village elder in Timnah. When my mother was a girl, my father and Grandpa Nabu came to Timnah each year to tell stories at the annual sheep-shearing festival. My mother watched from dawn to dusk in fascination and memorized their tales. At her own home, she acted out these stories for her family. She perfected her renditions of the goddesses Anat and Shaphash by practicing in front of her younger brothers and sisters. Soon, her brothers and sisters took on the roles of shepherds, maidservants, and minor gods in her plays.

One year at the sheep-shearing festival, my mother trailed behind my father and Grandpa Nabu. She pestered them until they agreed to watch her act. She vividly portrayed the sun goddess Shaphash holding court. My father said that he fell in love with my mother at that very instant. The next day, as my father and Grandpa Nabu told their stories at the festival, my mother pantomimed the actions of the characters. Crowds gathered around the trio and enthusiastically threw coins into Grandpa Nabu's basket.

By the time the sheep-shearing festival had ended, my mother and father were betrothed. A year later, they married and my mother became the lead actress of my father's and Grandpa Nabu's new pantomime troupe. Her parents allowed her to marry my father on two conditions. She must never act the part of a harlot, and every year, my father must bring her back to Timnah to visit them. My parents had kept both promises.

We visited many festivals and shrines each year. Although my father and Grandpa Nabu might skip the harvest celebration in Succoth or the seafarers' holy day in Phoenicia, they planned many moons in advance for the Timnah festival. Besides allowing my father to keep his promise to my mother's parents, my grandmother Arinna and grandfather Kothar, the festival was joyous and profitable.

My mother was the most talented actress in our troupe. She could act any role, but in keeping with her parents' wishes, she refused to play a harlot or temptress. She called these roles beneath her dignity and left them to the two other actresses in the troupe. Neither Rani nor Inbal objected to donning the costumes of prostitutes or seductive goddesses.

Rani and Inbal were both unmarried. They shared a tent, which my mother forbade me from entering. Rani stood tall and thin, with dark skin and high cheekbones, while Inbal was plump and large-breasted. Only Rani, when she danced in the crimson veil and purple-beaded tunic of a harlot, could enchant audiences like my mother. In each city where we stayed, Rani and Inbal drank wine with young shepherds and entertained traveling merchants. They joked around the campfire late into the night with Enten and Lahar, the two actors in our troupe. I envied their freedom. Sometimes, I would sit with them by the campfire and sip Lahar's barley beer if I knew my parents were not looking. While the fire still burned brightly and before the jokes grew too crude, my parents would call me into our tent to sleep.

The last time we performed in Bethel, Rani and Inbal invited me into their tent while my parents did business in the market. Tempted, I disregarded my parents' rules and followed them inside. Costumes, makeup, jewelry, and pillows cluttered the ground. Panels of crimson silk hung around each sleeping mat like canopies providing privacy. Rani saw me staring at her harlot costume lying on a camel bag.

"Do you want to try it on?" she asked. I picked up the fine fabric and held it in front of me.

"My mother would disapprove," I replied softly, handing it back to Rani.

"Your mother will not know," Rani said. "Besides, you will not be wearing it in public."

I put on the crimson veil.

"You are alluring. Look at yourself," Rani said, handing me her mirror.

I could discern only the outline of my eyes, nose, and lips in the mirror's copper face, but could feel my cheeks flush. I pulled the veil off and handed it back to Rani.

She laughed at me and taunted, "You need not be scared of a piece of fabric and a mirror."

Just then, I heard camels returning to camp, and then my parents' voices. Hastily, I ran out of Rani and Inbal's tent. It was too late. My parents had witnessed my escape.

"You know that you are forbidden from entering that tent," my mother said sharply. "They may choose to live a sordid life, but you are more respectable. One does not need to entertain men to be an actress. I both act and live respectably. When you are older, you will understand."

I wanted to retort that I was old enough to know how Rani and Inbal entertained men in their tent, but such a response would be far too disrespectful.

"Your mother is just looking out for your reputation," my father added to calm me.

"I apologize for disobeying you," I said meekly.

Our next stop after Bethel, luckily, was Timnah. There, we stayed at Grandmother Arinna's and Grandfather Kothar's home, and I had a break from Rani and Inbal. They did not stay with us in Timnah, for my mother worried that they might offend her parents. Rani, Inbal, Lahar, and Enten pitched their tents on the outskirts of town in a small village called Enaim. We saw them only at the sheep-shearing festival. Staying at my grandparents' house was a luxury. I slept in a bed rather than on the ground. My mother and I cooked the family meals on an indoor stove rather than a campfire.

"May I rehearse for a lead role at Timnah next year?" I asked my father, after my mother had put the final touches on my Egyptian princess outfit. "I am almost 15 and ready to play more than slave girls and princesses."

Before my father could answer, my mother said, "Perhaps your father and I should speak with you before making plans, Tamar."

My father nodded and sat down on a stool.

My mother continued, "Your father and I have discussed your future. We do not wish you to live a traveling life forever. Your prospects for marriage would be limited. Instead of marrying a wealthy merchant or shepherd, your destiny might be a poor actor like Enten or Lahar. Besides, in the past several moons, you have been tempted by . . ."

My father interrupted my mother and said, "I have spoken to Grandfather Kothar and Grandmother Arinna. Like us, they wish to see you marry well. You could stay here in Timnah with them and establish a dignified reputation for yourself."

I felt tears running down my face. "I do not wish to leave you," I said. "I like to perform. As Grandpa Nabu says, sharing tales is a holy duty. I will stay away from Rani and Inbal."

"We need not decide anything now," said my mother. "The Timnah festival lasts more than a week."

My father nodded in agreement and said, "In the meantime, I will give you a more important role right here at the festival. A group of Egyptian traders have arrived in town. I plan to tell a few lighthearted Egyptian legends for them. Would you like to play the dwarf god Bes? Enten, Lahar, and Rani are too tall for the part, and Inbal is too busty. Besides, I know that the stage transforms you into a comic."

I chuckled at the thought of imitating Bes with his bowlegs and protruding tongue. "It would be my pleasure," I answered.

The next day, after only one rehearsal, I danced in front of the audience with my knees facing outward. I wore a beard and bushy tail made from fleece, but a tight tunic so the audience would know that I was a girl. When I stuck my tongue out at the crowd, everybody laughed. I grinned and shook a tambourine in my hand. In the crowd, I noticed a man who laughed so hard that his eyes welled up with tears. After the show, he approached my father and me and put several coins in our basket.

"My name is Judah," said the man, smiling. "My friend Hirah and I appreciated your humor and your daughter's comedic skill. I tire of epics about war, conflict, and violence."

"I suggest, then, that you do not watch my wife's rendition of Anat. It is my next story," replied my father. "She is the finest of our actresses, but her performance erupts with rage."

"I know rage far too well," said Judah quietly.

The next day, Judah and Hirah returned to watch me act the part of Bes again. After my father finished telling the legend, Judah approached him to invite our family to a feast that evening at his home. When Judah said that he had three unmarried sons, my father quickly accepted the invitation.

Other than my costumes, I owned two outfits, one for traveling and one for celebrations and feasts. I smoothed out the wrinkles in the finer tunic and jacket and admired their deep purple color and gold needlework before putting them on. My mother braided my hair in plaits and dabbed a bit of makeup onto my face. I looked into our mirror and felt good about my reflection.

Judah sent a servant to lead my parents, Grandpa Nabu, and me to his home in the wilderness. Our camels followed the guide, carefully climbing down the path that led from Timnah to the pastures below. When we passed

Enaim, I saw Inbal and Rani sitting near the road with two shepherds. I recognized one of the shepherds as Judah's friend Hirah. I began to call to them, but stopped when my mother pretended not to notice them.

The setting sun cast a lavender and pink glow across the desert. Soon, we could no longer see Timnah and Enaim. We traveled until only a few rays of sunset were left on the horizon. Judah and his family lived in a compound of several houses surrounded by a protective wall. The compound was built in a small oasis. Around the oasis, the desert was spotted with bramble, juniper, and hyssop bushes. The outlines of mountains were barely visible in the distance.

Judah hurried out of the largest house, followed by three boys and an elderly man. "Welcome to my home," Judah said warmly. "I have told my family how you entertain audiences with stories and humor. Come, meet my father-in-law, Shua, and my sons, Er, Onan, and Shelah."

The tallest boy, the one named Er, looked a little older than me. He had shaggy brown hair that fell to his shoulders and a strong jaw line. Er bowed down before me. When nobody but me could see his face, he grinned. My heart beat quickly. Next, Onan walked forward. Onan's cheeks were covered with acne, and his forehead shone like olive oil. He kicked at the dirt and bowed. Then, Shelah walked forward and bowed in an exaggerated, grandiose style.

"Shelah just turned nine and enjoys being the jokester. He would join your acting troupe if I let him," said Judah. "My wife, Alit, and her maidservant have almost finished the meal. Let the servants bathe your feet. You can rest in my home until we eat."

I could tell that Judah's hospitality impressed my mother and father. Alit greeted us at the door and invited us to sit down on low chairs luxuriously covered with pillows. Er led me to a chair in the corner and sat on a stool next to me. The maidservant poured wine into glazed pottery goblets for us.

"In the tradition of my family, I offer a prayer," Judah proclaimed, raising his cup. "Blessed is the God of Sarah and Abraham for creating the fruit of the vine."

I had never heard of such a god. Grandpa Nabu looked curiously at Judah.

"The God of Sarah and Abraham? I have heard those names before," he said slowly, as though searching his memory. "Was your family the clan responsible for the massacre at Shechem?"

Each year, when we passed the deserted city of Shechem in our travels, Grandpa Nabu told the same story. Before I was born, a girl had been kidnapped and brought to Shechem by the prince of the city. In revenge, the girl's distraught brothers had slain all the men of the city.

"My sister, Dinah, was the girl kidnapped," said Judah awkwardly. "My brothers Simeon and Levi avenged the attack. I disapprove of their violence."

"I have thought of retelling your family's tale for audiences. It has become a legend of the land," said Grandpa Nabu.

"I try not to talk about what happened in Shechem. I have moved as far as possible from that city," said Judah. "I prefer more joyful topics."

"What happened to your sister?" I blurted out. My mother glared at me for speaking without being asked.

"Dinah left Canaan after the attack, for she feared retribution," Judah said. "My family believes that she went to Phoenicia and escaped on a boat." A maidservant began serving a meal of veal, dumpling stew, and fresh cucumbers mixed with dill.

"We should talk of happier matters, like your adventures as storytellers or finding matches for our lovely children," Judah said, looking at Er and me.

The men talked well into the night. The maidservant refilled their wine goblets many times. As the time to leave approached, my mother and I helped Alit and the maidservant clear away the dishes. When we walked outside, a full moon and a sky of stars had replaced the setting sun. Er put his hand on the small of my back and helped me onto my camel.

"I enjoyed meeting you, Tamar," he said.

On the way back to Timnah, Father and Grandpa Nabu talked eagerly about the idea of including the story of Dinah and Shechem in their repertoire of legends. My mother, who was sitting behind me on the camel, whispered, "Er was certainly polite. Did you think he was handsome?"

"Do not ask me such questions," I snapped in embarrassment. In truth, I could not stop thinking about Er's face or his touch on my back. I prayed that I would see him again before we left Timnah.

The next morning, Grandmother Arinna served us grape tarts and yogurt. "I heard that you met a good-looking and respectable young man last night," she said. "I look forward to meeting him and his family."

"When will you meet them?" I asked in surprise.

"Your father asked that we host them at our house tomorrow night. Did he not tell you?" she answered. "We sent a servant with the invitation at the break of dawn. The young man might prove to be a good match for you, my child. Besides, it is only proper to return their hospitality."

My parents' rush to invite Er and his family to my grandparents' home both delighted and frightened me.

My grandmother said to me, "Your mother tells me that you have only one fine outfit, and you wore it last night. I want to purchase another outfit for you as a gift."

My mother had always sewn my clothing, for only wealthy families purchased garments. As my grandmother and I walked to the city market, I imagined looking into my mirror and seeing a girl of prominence looking back. Grandmother Arinna led me to a stall full of tunics and jackets. I fingered through crimson, copper, scarlet, and indigo outfits folded neatly on top of one another. My eyes rested on a fine wool tunic, striped with different shades of purple murex. Silver threads decorated the neckline. I held the tunic up to my body and peered into a mirror that my grandmother held. The merchant brought me a solid purple jacket with silver embroidery. As I tried the jacket on, I pictured myself greeting Er at the door of my grandparents' home. Grandmother Arinna bartered for the outfit, exchanging a pair of gold earrings that Grandfather Kothar had crafted.

Er and his family arrived before dusk the following night. Er blushed slightly when he saw me and bowed. I giggled and showed him inside, patting down my new tunic as we walked. I sat next to Er and served him throughout the evening. My palms felt damp as I concentrated on not spilling food on Er or myself.

At the end of the meal, my mother asked me to help slice fruit for dessert. I listened from the next room as my father and Judah spoke.

"My son Er would like to marry your Tamar," Judah said. "Your daughter's charm has enchanted him. Would a match interest you? I am prepared to give a generous bride-price."

"Tamar is quite dear to her mother and me," my father responded. "We have a traveling life, as you know. Would your family watch over her?"

"We would be honored to have Tamar join our household. I would treat her as a daughter," Judah answered. "My family trusts in the God of Sarah and Abraham. Tamar would become a daughter of our traditions."

My mother put her arms around me as we listened to the men. I imagined kissing Er on our wedding night. Then I remembered that I would leave behind my family.

As if he knew of my hesitation, Judah said, "Following our God is a holy task. Tamar would share in this important role."

"Er and Tamar will make a fine pair," my father responded. "Let us call back the women to announce Er and Tamar's betrothal."

As I walked back into the room, I saw the desire on Er's face. I tried to hide my own yearnings.

"Tamar, my dear daughter, I have arranged for you to marry Er, the son of Judah and Alit," my father said proudly. "In the tradition of his family, let us thank the God of Sarah and Abraham for this moment."

Er rose from his chair and walked over to me. He placed a large gold bracelet on my wrist. He let his hand linger for a moment on my own. A warm sensation ran through my body.

My father and Judah arranged the details of our betrothal. I would travel with my parents for three moons to allow Er to prepare for my arrival at his family's home. We would marry at Judah's compound and live in a room that Judah and Er would build onto the back of their house.

The moons leading up to our wedding passed quickly. At each festival and shrine, I pantomimed my roles as Bes and the Egyptian princess, yet felt passion when I thought of Er. When our wedding finally came, my family's small caravan traveled first to Timnah. I tried on the wedding tunic that my mother had worn. It fit perfectly. Grandmother Arinna allowed me to choose my favorite of her jewelry to wear. She and Grandfather Kothar joined our caravan, and together we journeyed to Judah's compound. My mother allowed Rani, Inbal, Lahar, and Enten to attend the wedding. For better or worse, they had been an important part of my childhood. As we entered Judah's valley, I was stunned to see it full of tents, camels, and people. Ten small camps formed a circle around one large central camp. Judah's compound stood close by.

"It appears that Judah's whole family has come for your wedding," Grandpa Nabu said, laughing. "I will have the opportunity to meet the infamous Simeon and Levi. Our visit will provide much material for our story of their sister's rape and their revenge."

Judah approached quickly on a camel. "I did not warn you that my clan numbers 70," Judah said, looking at our caravan of 10 people.

"The rest of our family and friends will travel from Timnah on the day of the wedding," my father said, sounding slightly embarrassed about the size of our caravan. "Still, we will number only 20 or 30." By the time we arrived at the compound and dismounted our camels, a crowd had gathered.

"Let me introduce you to my family," Judah said. "First, my father, Jacob, and my mother, Leah." An elderly man and woman stepped forward. The woman had a veil over her face, but she lifted it to look at me. Her eyes were disfigured and gruesome. I told myself not to cringe. She smiled and bowed.

In succession, Judah introduced his stepmothers, Bilhah and Zilpah, and his 10 brothers. I heard names like Reuben, Asher, Dan, Issachar, and Zebulun and worried that I would never tell them apart. I tried not to stare when Simeon and Levi walked forward together. Lastly, Judah introduced his youngest brother, Benjamin. Benjamin was far closer in age to Er than to Judah.

Judah's father, Jacob, asked to speak. "It delights me that my family has gathered to witness the marriage of my grandson," Jacob said, beginning to cry. "It only sorrows me that my beloved wife Rachel and son Joseph cannot share in our joy. Death has taken them both."

Judah tensed up when their father mentioned the name Joseph. All his brothers cast their eyes toward the ground. I looked at my mother, and she shrugged. Judah put his arm around his father and embraced him gently.

"Let us focus on the joyful, Father," Judah said. "Auntie Rachel and Joseph would not want your tears."

With Judah's words, his brothers began to disperse. Er and Benjamin stayed behind and stood close together, talking quietly. Benjamin slapped Er playfully on the back. Er's and my eyes locked for just a moment. I smiled and quickly looked down. I heard them laugh. I noticed Onan walking away alone.

Judah brought my family to a small house within their compound. "You will be comfortable here," Judah said. "It is our servants' home, but they will stay in tents for the wedding week."

My mother told me that a bride does not show herself before her wedding. For the two days leading up the wedding, I would stay in the house. I could hear singing and laughing late into the night. My father and Grandpa Nabu told me that they entertained Jacob's family with their stories. Inbal, Rani, Lahar, and Enten took on roles, but my mother thought it immodest to act in front of her future in-laws. My mother stayed with me during the celebrations. My grandmother and Alit often joined us.

The evening before my wedding, I lay on the bed and listened to the party outside. When I could not sleep, I climbed up to the roof to watch. In the distance, I recognized Rani's and Inbal's tent. I felt jealous that they could participate in the celebrations for my wedding and I could not. Just then, I noticed two men walk out of their tent. I could see only the outlines of their bodies. I told myself that my eyes were deceiving me, that these shadows were not Er and Benjamin.

The next morning, my mother and grandmother took me to bathe. I wanted to tell them about the shadows leaving Rani and Inbal's tent, but I feared their reaction. I donned the family wedding tunic, and my mother braided my hair. She gently applied makeup to my face. This time, I did not fidget. Before I put on the veil, I peered into my copper mirror. I saw a bride looking back and felt fear and joy brimming within me.

Under a wedding canopy, Er lifted my veil tenderly. I saw in his eyes that he wanted me, and I felt ashamed that I had distrusted him. He nodded to his father and took my hand. I looked down modestly, as a proper bride should. It would be several hours until Er and I were alone.

After the wedding, I was able to participate in the festivities. Alit, my mother, and the other women took my hands, and we danced in circles until I could hardly stand. Servants brought platter after platter of veal, vegetables, breads, and fruits for us to eat. Alit handed me a pomegranate. She told me that eating its mass of seeds encouraged fertility. When Inbal danced next to me, she whispered not to fear my wedding night.

After most of Judah's family had retired to their tents, my mother and father hugged me. Er took my hand and led me to the room that would be our home. That night and for many nights afterward, Er and I shared our passion for one another. He was kind and gentle. We talked as much as we made love.

A week after our wedding, Judah's family took down their tents and returned to their home in Kirith-arba. The valley seemed quiet, almost empty. That night, I asked Er why his father had not settled near his brothers.

Er answered slowly, as if uncertain of how much to share. "My father is a jovial man. He detests violence and bloodshed. He craves only a world at peace. His brothers are not like him. They can be quarrelsome and even vicious."

"I know about Dinah's kidnapping and Simeon's and Levi's attack on Shechem," I replied.

"My father worried that your father might reject our marriage because of what happened in Shechem," Er said. "There is more that you do not know. My father had another brother, named Joseph. My grandfather Jacob favored Joseph and spoiled him. Once, my father and his brothers were herding sheep far from home. My grandfather sent Joseph to find them. While Joseph was searching for them, a wild beast attacked him. My father and his brothers found his jacket torn and bloody. My father has always felt responsible. He left his father's house a short time later and married my mother."

"How did your father and mother meet?" I asked.

"My mother was Dinah's best friend," Er answered. "My father thought she would understand his history and sought her out. My parents wanted to escape their bad memories, so they followed their friend Hirah south to Timnah."

I cuddled up in Er's arms and said, "The more I learn about you, the more I feel at home."

I cried only slightly when my parents packed their belongings to leave. As I hugged them good-bye, my father said that they would see me in a year when they returned to Timnah.

But, less than one moon after our wedding, Er fell ill. I awoke one morning to find the blanket on our bed damp with perspiration. Er trembled next to me in bed, his face red and his eyes watery.

"Tamar, my head feels like fire," he whispered.

I kissed his forehead and felt the fever through my lips. I ran for Alit and Judah. They brought water-soaked rags and washed Er's face. I sat next to him and prayed to the God of Sarah and Abraham. Er could not eat and could hardly drink. On the third night of his illness, he coughed up blood. Judah sent for his mother, for she was a medicine woman. As the days passed, Er grew weaker. Alit and I sat by his side day and night. Soon, Er slept more than he was awake. On the seventh morning, after Alit left to draw water for him, Er awoke and looked at me.

"Is my mother in the room?" he asked weakly.

"No," I answered, caressing his arm and drawing closer. "We are alone."

"I fear the God of Sarah and Abraham is punishing me," he whispered. "I was frightened before our wedding that I would not please you. Benjamin brought me to Inbal and Rani's tent. They showed me how to kiss you. They offered to show me more, but I refused. Still, you deserved more loyalty."

"You have pleased me," I assured him. "I have found my passion in you."

"Tamar, have a child for me," Er said with more strength. "Then I will live on."

"I promise. I will," I said, crying.

Er had closed his eyes and fell asleep. The next morning, he died. His grandmother Leah arrived with her chest of medicines that afternoon.

Grandfather Kothar and Grandmother Arinna came from Timnah for the funeral. My grandmother had purchased a widow's tunic and veil from the same merchant we had visited less than six moons before. I peered into my mirror and was taken aback by my image. Judah buried Er in a cave just beyond his compound. Alit wailed uncontrollably. I patted my belly and prayed that I was pregnant.

At the next full moon, though, my period of women came. When I felt the first familiar cramp, Er was truly dead for me. I told Alit, and tears flowed from her eyes. She, too, had prayed that I might bear Er's child. The next morning, Judah and Alit approached me.

"You are still able to give Er a legacy," Judah said. "Marry Onan. Your first child together will be considered Er's heir. Er's death has brought only pain and sorrow. If you bear an heir for Er, perhaps all of us will find some peace."

I felt nothing but distaste for Onan. But I was devoted to Er's memory and my promise of bearing a child for him, so I agreed. Without festivity, I married Onan. My parents were traveling and did not know. Only Grandfather Kothar and Grandmother Arinna attended, and they cried quietly at the ceremony.

Onan moved into the room I had shared with Er. We tried to talk, but our words were awkward. I felt no passion for Onan, and I doubt that he felt passion for me. We attempted to kiss, but it too was uncomfortable. At night, we slept as far as possible from one another on the bed where Er had died.

"Onan, I know that you do not love me," I said. "But you did love your brother, and we can have a child in his name."

"My brother meant little to me," Onan said. "With his good looks and status as elder, he had everything and I had nothing. I have no desire to give a child to his memory."

One moon after our wedding, Onan woke up with an all-too-familiar fever. I sat next to him like a dutiful wife, but when I held his hand, he pulled it away. He died in just three days, not seven. I put on my widow's garb once again and sat in mourning, this time for a husband that I did not love.

My period of women came the next week. Judah and Alit knew that again I had not given them a grandchild. For a full week, Judah did not speak to me. I knew that now he blamed me for his sons' deaths. I blamed myself as well. I wondered if I had struck Er and Onan with a curse.

"Give Judah time to heal," Alit told me. "He thinks of you as a daughter, but he feels that death might follow you. He despises sorrow yet has known it often."

After an awkward seven days of silence, Judah came to me. He asked me to sit down.

"Tamar, for now, I have no more sons to give you," Judah said. "Shelah is still young and will not be ready to marry for several years. I, myself, would marry you and have children in my sons' names. I am strong and could combat any curse. But my father had more than one wife and I witnessed the jealousy it caused. I will not impose such unpleasantness on Alit, for she has suffered enough."

I gasped at the thought of marrying Judah, even though such a union could provide a child in Er's name. I had few options. Until I married again, I was destined to wear a widow's tunic and veil. No young man would want me now that I had had two husbands die within a moon of marriage. Besides, I was still bound to Er's family.

Judah broke into my thoughts. "I have sent a servant to find your father and bring him to us. You will stay as a widow in your father's house until my son Shelah grows up."

My parents and Grandpa Nabu arrived a few weeks later. My mother saw me in a widow's outfit and fell to the ground. She clasped me around the knees and began to wail. Alit prepared a simple meal of bread and lentil soup. We ate silently. Before dusk, I prepared to leave with my parents.

"You will send a servant to find us when Shelah reaches the age of marriage?" my father asked.

"Yes," Judah said awkwardly, looking down as he spoke.

Alit hugged me and wished me well.

Being free of Judah's compound was refreshing. Although I still wore my widow's garb, I was relieved not to live amid constant sorrow. My parents gave me my own small tent. My mother said that it was not appropriate for a widow to sleep in the same tent as her parents. For many moons, we did not discuss my future.

As we prepared for our annual visit in Timnah, I asked my parents if I could camp in Enaim with the other actors. I could not bear to stay in the home where Er and I had become betrothed. On eve of the sheep-shearing festival, Lahar, Enten, and I sat around the campfire talking. Lahar told a joke that made me laugh for the first time since Er's death.

During the Timnah festival, I wore my widow's garb and watched my father and Grandpa Nabu tell stories. Only one year before, I had donned a tail and beard and portrayed Bes. I tried to remember the audience's laughter. The people of Timnah knew I had had two husbands die within three moons. I heard them whisper words like "curse," "tragic," and "child widow." I attempted to ignore them.

Years passed slowly. I asked my parents if I could begin to act again. My mother told me that it was inappropriate for a young widow. I told her that I understood, and surprisingly, I did. Besides, I had passion for only one purpose, bearing a child in Er's name. Each year when we arrived in Timnah, my father sent either Lahar or Enten to Judah's compound to inquire about Shelah. Each year, Judah said that Shelah was still too young to marry.

Five years after Er's death, my father sent Enten to check on Shelah when we arrived in Timnah for the annual festival. Enten reported that, once again, Judah had said Shelah was too young to marry. But this year, Enten had tragic news as well. Alit had passed away six moons before. I mourned Alit, regretting that I had not provided a grandchild for her before she died.

That evening as we camped in Enaim, Rani and Inbal invited me into their tent. They said that we needed to speak.

"Enten did not tell everything to your father," Rani began. "He saw Shelah, and Shelah has grown up. He is a young man, certainly of marriageable age. Your father-in-law has tricked you. He has no intention of letting you marry his last son."

I had already suspected what Rani confirmed. Judah feared losing another son to me and would keep us apart forever, if possible. I would remain a widow for life. Worse yet, I would not fulfill my promise to Er to bear a child in his name.

Inbal put her arm around me and said, "Tamar, we consider you to be our younger sister. We despise watching you grow old in this depressing widow's garb. We miss your laughter and joy. It is time for you to take charge and to act."

Rani said, "We have a plan. Judah's friend Hirah visited us last night. In passing, he told us that Judah has just finished mourning Alit. Tomorrow evening, Hirah will bring him to Timnah to find a harlot for a little female companionship."

Inbal continued where Rani ended, "Take off your widow's garb and wear Rani's harlot costume. If you sit by the side of the road, Judah will see you when he goes to Timnah. He will assume that you are a harlot, just the type of woman he seeks. If you conceive a child by Judah, then you will be free from your widow's garb and also provide a child in Er's memory."

I sat in shock as I listened to their scheme. I could not imagine wearing Rani's harlot costume as an actress, let alone truly playing the part and seducing my father-in-law.

"The plan you suggest is disgraceful," I said. "I could not do anything so loathsome."

"Playing a harlot may not be enviable," Rani said. "But neither is spending the rest of your life as a widow."

"Judah has been dishonorable to you and to Er's memory," Inbal said. "For the past five years, you have talked of nothing but your desire to provide an heir for Judah's firstborn son. You would not be seducing Judah, but reclaiming your rights as his daughter-in-law."

I could not sleep that night. I agonized over Rani and Inbal's words. The more I considered their plan, the more I saw wisdom in it. Judah had trapped me as a widow. I had promised his son, my beloved Er, a child. I could no longer offend Alit; rather, I would provide a child in her memory. By morning, I had convinced myself to do the unthinkable—to accept the part of a harlot.

Rani and Inbal helped me dress. The veil distorted my identity. I wrapped it so it hugged my body. When I looked in my mirror, I struggled to see myself as respectable.

That evening, Enten and Lahar stood guard by the road to signal when Judah and Hirah approached. When Enten blew a ram's horn twice, I walked out of the tent and sat by the side of the road. A few moments later, Judah and Hirah rode toward me on camels.

When Hirah saw me, he said, "Judah, I told you that there would be women to entertain you. Go, talk to this harlot. Perhaps she will bring you comfort."

Judah dismounted the camel. He said nervously, "Let me sleep with you."

As Inbal and Rani had coached me, I responded, "What will you pay me?" I surprised myself with the boldness of my voice.

He responded, "I will send a goat from my flock."

"Should I believe you?" I said. "You must give me a pledge that I will be paid."

"What pledge should I give you?" Judah said.

I searched within me and found the confidence to demand Judah's most important identification. I asked for his seal and cord, which he used to stamp his signature, and his shepherd's staff, which was personally carved for him. I was stunned when he agreed.

Judah followed me to my tent. I thought only of Er when Judah lay with me. After he left, I returned the harlot's costume to Rani and dressed again in my widow's garb. I cried all night. Rani and Inbal tried to comfort me, but I ignored them.

The next morning, I sought out my parents. "I wish to stay with Grandfather Kothar and Grandmother Arinna in Timnah," I said. "I have tired of traveling. Besides, they have grown elderly and frail and could use my assistance."

"I thought that you wished to avoid your grandparents' home, for you and Er were betrothed there," my father answered.

"Time has passed," I explained. "Perhaps I will feel closer to Er in their home."

"Your plan makes sense," said my mother. "If you stay in Timnah, Judah will be able to find you quickly when Shelah is ready to marry."

When the sheep-shearing festival ended, I moved into my grandparents' home. I helped my grandmother Arinna with her daily chores and cleaned up my grandfather Kothar's workshop each evening. I tried not to think of my future.

Walking through the market one morning, I passed several of the town elders whispering and laughing. I thought nothing of their revelry until I heard the name "Hirah the Adullamite." I pretended to inspect cucumbers at a vegetable booth so I could listen. Two of the men recounted that Hirah had approached them and asked about a harlot to whom he owned a goat as payment. Hirah insisted that the woman existed although nobody else had ever seen her. In the following days, I listened for more gossip about Hirah and the missing harlot but heard none. I assumed that Hirah and Judah were worried about being the laughingstock of the town. I was relieved that they gave up searching.

One moon passed, then another. My period of women did not come. By the fourth moon, my belly began to swell. My grandparents' eyes were weak with old age, and they did not realize that I was pregnant. I heard the townsfolk gossiping about me. I realized that, soon enough, Judah would hear the news.

One evening, Judah appeared at our door with several town elders.

"Tamar has played the harlot. She is rightfully married into my family yet has given herself to somebody else, perhaps even for payment," Judah said when Grandfather Kothar opened the door. "She must be brought out and burned for her dishonor."

I grabbed Judah's seal, cord, and staff and hid them in my tunic. Grandfather Kothar gasped with horror as town guards clasped my arms and carried me out to the market. My heart beat quickly. I trembled. If the scheme did not work, I knew my fate. I told myself to trust that Judah was a fair, if frightened, man. By the city market, a small crowd gathered around Judah, the town elders, and me.

The chief elder of Timnah asked, "Do you have a defense for this dishonorable act? If so, speak."

I held out the seal, cord, and staff and handed them to Judah.

"I am with child by the man to whom these belong," I said. "Examine them."

The elders crowded around Judah. Judah took a single look at the items and stepped backward in shock. He did not speak. The elders continued to examine the items. The chief elder knew Judah well and recognized the items also. He looked straight at Judah with a piercing stare.

"The items are mine," Judah confessed. "She is more in the right than I, inasmuch as I did not give her to my son Shelah."

I sighed deeply and patted my belly. My grandmother Arinna and grandfather Kothar ran up to me. The crowd began to whisper. "Go back to your homes," the chief elder said to the crowd.

Soon Judah, my grandparents, and I were alone.

"How could you ask for Tamar's death?" Grandfather Kothar said sternly. "At one time, you loved her as a daughter. You have always told us that you detest violence."

"I was confused by grief," Judah said weakly. "Tamar, forgive me. Please come live in my compound. Let me help you raise our child. I will treat you with the fairness that you deserve."

"My baby belongs to Er, not you," I replied. "I will live with my grandparents, if they will have me. You may visit your grandchild." My grandparents put their arms around me and guided me back to their home.

Five moons later, I gave birth to twin boys. During my labor, one baby put out his hand. The midwife tied a red thread around his wrist to signify that he was the firstborn. He retracted his hand and let his brother come out.

"You are eager for the world, just like your father Er," I said. "I will call you Perez. May you bring peace to my world." A moment later, I gave birth to the baby with the crimson thread on his wrist. "Welcome, my son. I will call you Zerah," I said, smiling. "Er and I had enough love for two sons."

"Hold up my mirror please, Grandmother," I said, cradling Perez in one arm and Zerah in the other. I peered into the mirror's copper face and saw my passion, my two sons, in its reflection.

Tamar takes her mirror and places it in Lilith's ark. Years pass, and Judah keeps his promise, treating her only with respect. When Judah and his family venture down to Egypt, she goes with them. There, she meets Dinah and her daughter Asenath. She gives the ark to Asenath and says, "I believe this ark now belongs to you."

Eventually, Perez and Zerah have children of their own. The line of Perez becomes the line of King David, and many say it will be the line of the Messiah, bringing peace to our world.

9 | ASENATH: THE GOLDEN NECKLACE

A HINT FROM TORAH:

Pharaoh then gave Joseph the name Zaphenath-paneah; and he gave him for a wife Asenath daughter of Poti-phera, priest of On....

GENESIS 41:45

The Torah tells us very little about Asenath. We learn only that her father is Poti-phera, she marries Joseph, and she gives birth to Manassah and Ephraim. Asenath's life is more fully developed in the *midrashim* of the ancient rabbis. The rabbis were disturbed that Joseph married an Egyptian and not a daughter of Israel. To solve this dilemma, the rabbis imagined Dinah becoming pregnant when Shechem raped her. The child of this rape is Asenath. As an infant, Asenath is sent to Egypt, where she is adopted. According to the *midrash*, her adoptive father, Poti-phera, who is also known as Potiphar, purchases Joseph when he arrives in Egypt. The name Asenath means "a favorite of the Egyptian goddess Neith." Although named for an Egyptian goddess, Asenath wears a golden charm inscribed "God of Israel" as a symbol of her true lineage. She feels connected to this ancestry even though she is raised as an Egyptian.

Let us meet Asenath...

To escape the tension between my two mothers, Zuleika and Dinah, I often sat next to the small pond in our family's courtyard. I listened to the gentle sounds of the flowing water and watched red carp swim peacefully among blue lotus flowers. The lotus flowers amazed me. Their petals closed in a small ball each evening and retreated underneath the water. Each morning, the flowers reappeared and slowly opened, revealing their long purple petals and brilliant golden centers. The flowers filled the air with sweet fragrance. Like every young person in Egypt, I knew that the lotus flower represented the sun forever changing as it moved across the sky. According to legend, the sun god Atum emerged from a lotus flower when he was born.

I thought the lotus flower could also represent me. I, too, changed with the time of day. During the day, I was Egyptian nobility and my parents were Zuleika and Potiphar. They adopted me because they were barren and pledged to transform me into a noble like them. At night, in the privacy of my room, I was a daughter of Israel and my mother was Dinah. Dinah gave birth to me and served as my nursemaid, as well as my confidante and closest friend.

As far back as I can remember, Mother Zuleika insisted that I would marry a royal advisor, a government official, or perhaps a physician. When I reached young adulthood, grooming me for this proper marriage became her obsession. Each day, she critiqued my clothing, makeup, and manners.

"Asenath, you have the coloring and hair of a Canaanite," she would tell me. "To conceal it, you must take extra care with your cosmetics and wigs."

I took lengthy daily lessons in reading, writing, and mathematics. Mudada, a kindly but elderly teacher from the local boys' school, tutored me. He often fell asleep as I did my writing exercises. When he began to snore, I poked him with a papyrus reed to wake him. I knew that if Mother Zuleika ever witnessed Mudada dozing off, she would reprimand him and call him lazy.

Mother Zuleika taught me the Book of Instruction herself. Every young member of the nobility studied its rules of behavior and obedience. Mother Zuleika was strict and moody. If my answers did not please her, she called me unworthy of learning.

"No young man of status will want a wife who is uncultured or illiterate," she answered me. "You come from a line of peasants, but I can make you into more."

Often, I went with Mother Zuleika to banquets or riverboat rides or *senet* games at the palace. She called these outings my training as an Egyptian noble-woman. My stomach churned with anxiety whenever I accompanied her, for she always critiqued my manners afterward.

As much as Mother Zuleika badgered me with her expectations and demands, she treated my mother Dinah far worse, taking every opportunity to criticize her.

"Your mother came to Egypt poor, pregnant, and without a husband," Mother Zuleika said. "We took pity on her when we adopted you and accept-ed her as a nursemaid."

Mother Zuleika knew that my mother was raped and fled Canaan in fear for her life and mine. It was futile to remind her.

Mother Zuleika and Potiphar provided me with a large bedroom appro-priate for the royal young woman that they expected me to become. My moth-er Dinah slept in a small, adjoining annex. In our rooms, we could talk freely with one another.

"Asenath, please understand that I was desperate when I allowed Zuleika to adopt you," my mother would tell me often. "My Aunt Rachel acted like my adoptive mother, raising me alongside my mother, Leah. I loved Rachel and trusted that Zuleika would be as kind to you."

Every night, I shared with my mother the lessons that Mudada had taught me. I knew that Mother Zuleika would be furious if she knew that my moth-er was learning to read and write.

"Learning from you is my one luxury," my mother said, smiling broadly. "Not even my father knew how to read."

My mother taught me about our family's unique legacy. Her family had its own God. The God of Sarah and Abraham had spoken to each generation of our ancestors, beginning with my great, great grandparents. As a small child, she gave me a gold charm inscribed with the words "God of Sarah and Abraham." I wore the charm on a long cord and hid it in my tunic. When I was nervous, I thought of the charm and imagined Sarah and Abraham having the confidence to follow their dreams.

"I want you to be proud of our lineage and traditions," my mother told me each night. "Mother Zuleika's words sting me less and less every day. Her insults about our family have become insignificant to me. But I worry about you, and certainly I cannot forgive her for Joseph, my dear brother."

Joseph's story haunted my mother. She repeated it time and time again, starting with their childhood in Canaan.

"Our father pampered Joseph, and our brothers knew it," my mother said. "God gave Joseph the skill of foreseeing the future and interpreting dreams. This gift only grew stronger as Joseph matured. Joseph did not ask to be able to predict the future, but our brothers held it against him. I must admit that Joseph could be arrogant, but he was just a young boy trying to impress his brothers."

A few years after my mother fled Canaan, her brothers, filled with jealousy, had had enough of Joseph. They sold him as a slave to traders traveling to Egypt.

By the divine touch of God, Potiphar bought Joseph and brought him home as a slave. Joseph and my mother were miraculously reunited. Wisely, they knew better than to reveal their relationship to Potiphar and Mother Zuleika. One afternoon, my mother returned from the market and found Joseph gone. Apparently, Joseph had insulted Mother Zuleika. In her fury, Mother Zuleika had Joseph sent to jail. A rumor spread that Joseph had kissed Mother Zuleika and, full of passion, had tried to push her onto her bed. My mother did not believe it. In the 12 years since Joseph's arrest, my mother had not heard from him.

Whenever somebody knocked at our door, my mother stopped her chores and looked up eagerly. She had faith that one day Joseph would reappear. I suspected that Joseph was dead, although I never told her my fears. I knew that she needed to hope.

One afternoon, not Joseph, but a royal chariot arrived at our home. A servant ushered the royal messenger inside. Mother Zuleika quickly appeared, for she had been expecting an invitation from Pharaoh's wife. Surprisingly, the messenger asked for my mother and me.

"Pharaoh requests the presence of Asenath and her nursemaid, Dinah, in the royal throne room," he proclaimed.

"Are you certain that Pharaoh asked for Dinah and not Zuleika?" asked Mother Zuleika in confusion. "What could Pharaoh possibly want with a simple servant?'"

"Pharaoh was specific," replied the messenger. "He said bring Asenath, her nursemaid, Dinah, and nobody else. Pharaoh's most trusted aide,

Zaphenath-paneah, saw the young woman at a banquet and was impressed with her. He wishes to meet her personally."

"It is highly irregular for Pharaoh to invite a young woman to the palace without her father or mother," said Mother Zuleika.

"Are you questioning Pharaoh's request?" said the messenger.

Mother Zuleika replied in a panic, "Of course not. I respect Pharaoh and his wisdom. When would Pharaoh like Asenath and Dinah to appear?"

"Immediately," said the messenger.

"But Asenath is not dressed appropriately to meet Pharaoh or even enter the royal palace. Certainly, he does not want to see a girl windblown from lessons in the courtyard," said Mother Zuleika. "Let her change her clothes and tidy her makeup and hair."

"Be quick," replied the messenger.

Mother Zuleika, my mother, and I ran to my bedroom. As Mother Zuleika chose my outfit, she muttered that Pharaoh would reprimand the messenger for not bringing her to the palace. Holding my golden charm tightly in my fist, I wondered anxiously what awaited me. Soon, I reappeared ready to meet Pharaoh and his aide. As the messenger led us to the chariot, I realized that my mother had not had time to change. She still wore her work clothes and no makeup or jewelry. I began to apologize, but she interrupted.

"It does not matter how I look, Asenath. They want to meet you, not me," she said.

A horse pulled the chariot swiftly to the palace. I had visited Pharaoh's palace several times for banquets. My mother, of course, had never been inside. She gasped as we entered the grand foyer with its ivory and gold furnishings. Murals dedicated to the gods covered the walls, and the floor had lapis lazuli stones imbedded among its tiles.

One of Pharaoh's officials met us and guided us to the throne room. Nobody could enter the throne room except by the invitation of Pharaoh himself. The room was long and narrow with columns lining its length and a raised platform at the end. A grand throne of gold, inlaid with gems, was positioned in the center of the platform. Pharaoh was sitting on the throne. The royal scribe and cupbearer stood off to the side. An official dressed in the finest linen clothing stood next to Pharaoh. Like the other officials, he wore black kohl on his eyes, a traditional wig, and a large collar made of gold and gemstones.

When we were close enough to see the men's faces clearly, my mother's body froze. She let out a small squeal. The official next to Pharaoh smiled just slightly and nodded at my mother.

"It cannot be," my mother whispered.

Before I could react, our guide called out, "As you have requested, I introduce Asenath, daughter of Zuleika and Potiphar, and her nursemaid, Dinah."

My mother and I bowed down low in front of the throne.

"Young woman," Pharaoh said to me. "The gods have entrusted my chief aide, Zaphenath-paneah, with the gift of dream interpretation. Less than one moon ago, he saw you at a royal banquet. Last night, he dreamt that Hathor, the love goddess, told him to marry you. Hathor commanded that you and your nursemaid move immediately into the palace. In exchange, Hathor promised that my sons will be lucky in love."

I stood speechless in front of Pharaoh. My mother touched my back to encourage me, but still I could not find any words.

"May I, your most loyal servant, speak?" said my mother finally, bowing once more. Pharaoh nodded.

"Asenath believes in the power of dreams. She is a faithful and educated girl meant for nobility," said my mother. "If the god Hathor visited your chief aide in his dreams and told him to marry Asenath, I feel certain that her parents would agree to the union."

"It is decided. In one moon's time, Zaphenath-paneah and Asenath will marry. May their union bring fortune to the palace," said Pharaoh. "Zaphenath-paneah, you may give gifts to Asenath as a sign of your betrothal."

My future husband stepped off the platform and approached me, but he looked at my mother. As he placed a ring on my finger, he whispered, "Dinah, it is me."

Pharaoh spoke. "I congratulate you on a wise choice of a bride. Asenath and her nursemaid should return to Potiphar's house at once and gather their belongings. My cupbearer will arrange for servants to move the women's belongings into the palace."

Pharaoh stood up and everybody bowed low to him as he too stepped off the platform. The scribe and cupbearer followed him out of the room, leaving my mother and me alone with Zaphenath-paneah. As soon as the room was empty, he embraced my mother.

"Joseph, is it truly you?" my mother cried out. "I prayed each day to our God that we would see each other again."

"Your eyes do not deceive you. I am Joseph," he said.

"But how?" my mother asked.

"Two moons ago, Pharaoh had a dream that he sought to understand. I was brought from prison to interpret it," Joseph said quickly and quietly, knowing we might be interrupted at any moment. "I listened to Pharaoh's dream and told him to prepare Egypt for seven years of plenty followed by seven years of famine. In gratitude, Pharaoh not only freed me from prison, but also made me a royal official. He told me to request any young woman in Egypt as my wife. At the last royal banquet, I saw Asenath sitting with Zuleika and knew immediately that she was my niece. When I learned she was available for marriage, I grasped the opportunity for us to reunite and for you to escape Zuleika's clutches. To ensure Pharaoh would not object, I told him that his favorite god had instructed me to marry Asenath."

Just then, two hefty servants walked into the throne room and bowed in front of Joseph.

"The cupbearer sent us to move these women into the palace," said one of the servants.

"Yes, of course," Joseph replied. Looking at me, he whispered, "We will have time to learn about one another later."

The same messenger who brought us to the palace took us back. The quick breeze of the chariot ride calmed my nerves. I could hardly grasp that I had met Joseph, let alone that I would marry him.

Mother Zuleika ran out of our house when she saw the chariot approach. Potiphar followed behind her.

The messenger proclaimed, "Pharaoh told his most trusted aide, Zaphenath-paneah, to select a wife from among the young women of Egypt. He has chosen Asenath, daughter of Zuleika and Potiphar. She and her nurse-maid will move into the palace tonight."

"My daughter will marry into the royal court," exclaimed Mother Zuleika, hugging me. "From your humble beginnings, I have raised you to marry a noble."

"I thank you for what you have provided me," I said in an attempt to be gracious. "Without everything you have done, Zaphenath-paneah certainly would not have chosen me as his wife."

"I will send word to Pharaoh's wife tomorrow that I wish to help in planning your wedding," said Mother Zuleika.

"Thank you, Mother Zuleika, but I suspect that your assistance will not be needed," I said.

Mother Zuleika stepped back in shock. My mother and I walked past her and into the house. When we were out of her earshot, we laughed and hugged one another. Quickly, we packed our belongings into a large chest.

My mother, who had been so calm at the palace, now looked stunned. She kept repeating, "Joseph has been released from prison. He is an aide to Pharaoh and your future husband."

"It is true," I reassured her. "We will leave Mother Zuleika's home. You no longer need to listen to her insults or do her chores."

We returned to the palace in the early hours of morning.

A servant greeted us at the door and said, "An army captain had a disturbing dream tonight. Zaphenath-paneah has been called away to interpret it. He instructed me to say that he wishes to spend time with Asenath in the morning."

The servant led us to our rooms. I was pleased that the two rooms were almost identical in size. Each room had a large, carved bed covered with fine white linen sheets and an ivory headrest. A maidservant appeared and helped us to unpack. Sleep came quickly when I climbed into bed.

The next morning, a different maidservant arrived with a meal of fruit, yogurt, and bread.

"Zaphenath-paneah wishes to meet you in the royal garden when you are ready," the maidservant said. "May I help you dress and put on your makeup?"

"Thank you, but it is not necessary," I replied. "I brought my nursemaid, and she will help me." Just then, my mother appeared at my door. Together, we chose a tunic for me to wear. She applied makeup gently to my face.

"Are you frightened to marry him?" my mother asked.

"My stomach is full of anxiety, and my heart is full of questions," I replied. "But I am also full of joy that we have been reunited and have left Mother Zuleika behind."

When I was ready, a maidservant led me through the palace and into the garden. I saw Joseph standing near a pomegranate tree, looking off into the distance. He turned before I approached.

"Asenath, you look stunning this morning," he said. "Let us walk through the garden and talk."

We walked down a path lined with red poppy flowers. An awkward silence fell between us. I saw a pond in the distance with blue lotus flowers floating on its surface.

When we arrived at the pond, I broke the silence and said, "Should I call you Joseph or Zaphenath-paneah?"

"Sometimes, I do not know which one I am," replied Joseph with a chuckle. "Although I appear Egyptian, I feel like a son of Israel. I pray out loud to Egyptian gods and silently to the God of Sarah and Abraham. "

"I know how you feel," I said. "I sometimes tell myself that I am like a lotus flower, constantly changing."

Joseph reached out and held my hands. He said, "I need to talk with you. I know that you probably do not want to marry a man twice your age. We can consider it to be a marriage of necessity, if you like. We need not be intimate."

"Do you view me as your niece or your future wife?" I asked.

"I am not sure," he said.

Exactly one moon later, Joseph and I were married according to the traditions of Egypt. For seven days leading up to the wedding, Pharaoh sponsored feasts in our honor. On the night before the wedding, an artisan painted henna on my hands and feet while women of the royal court sang songs praising my beauty. My anger toward Mother Zuleika had begun to lessen, and I invited her to the henna ceremony. She sat proudly next to me.

"Look how I raised Asenath for nobility and culture," Mother Zuleika boasted to anybody who would listen.

On the morning of the wedding, my mother braided my hair and helped me dress in the finery of a royal bride. I embraced her. Since the whole palace believed her to be my nursemaid, she watched the ceremony with the rest of the servants. Mother Zuleika and Potiphar stood with me. Joseph surprised me by having blue lotus flowers spread over the platform on which we wed. When the ceremony ended, all the nobles threw green wheat at us. It was a sign of fertility. The celebration of our marriage lasted well into the night.

Members of the royal court sang songs of passion when they escorted Joseph and me to the bridal room for our wedding night. Little did they know that my mother was waiting inside the room. When the door closed behind us, she emerged from her hiding spot. Joseph embraced my mother and me at the same time. Then we joined hands.

Together, we said, "Blessed is the God of Sarah and Abraham for reuniting us and making us a family once again."

For many moons, Joseph visited my room at night, although we were not intimate. At first, we simply did not want the servants to question our marriage. But we grew to truly enjoy one another's company. We talked late into the night. I found myself eagerly awaiting sunset each evening so I could see Joseph again.

One night, Joseph said, "I have an answer to your question."

"Which question?" I responded in puzzlement.

"You asked me if I see you as my wife or my niece. I see you as my wife, and I crave you," he answered, reaching over to kiss me.

I allowed Joseph to kiss me, but I stopped him before he did anything more.

"I need more time," I said.

"I will be patient," he replied.

Slowly, I felt the passion for Joseph that he felt for me. Our marriage of necessity evolved into a marriage of love.

The morning after we were first intimate, I said to Joseph, "You are a thoughtful and patient man. I thank you for waiting for me."

"I was not always patient, but 12 years in prison changed me," Joseph said. Then, he laughed, "Besides, remember I have the gift of foreseeing the future. I knew that, eventually, you would choose to love me."

Our marriage was a happy one. Before our fourth anniversary, I had given birth to two sons, Manasseh and Ephraim. Our boys learned with the other children of the palace. The best teachers in Egypt taught them. In public, our family prayed to the gods of Egypt. Everybody knew Joseph came from Canaan. Nobody suspected that I had anything but Egyptian ancestry or that Dinah was not my nursemaid but my mother. Behind closed doors, Joseph and I taught our sons to praise the God of Sarah and Abraham. We told them to be proud of our family's secret legacy.

After her servitude to Mother Zuleika, my mother could finally relax. As my mother aged, I watched her grow younger in appearance, not older. In the mornings, she helped me dress to maintain the guise of being a nursemaid.

Then, she played with her grandsons, tended to flowers in the royal gardens, or painted murals with the palace artists. In all our years in Mother Zuleika's house, she had never told me that she was a talented artist as a young woman.

Just as Joseph predicted, Egypt's fields and orchards yielded plentiful grain, vegetables, and fruit for seven years. In the eighth year, the rainy season did not come, the Nile did not overflow its banks, and the land stopped producing harvests. Because Joseph had advised Pharaoh to prepare for this famine, there was enough food for the people. Pharaoh rewarded Joseph by giving us a fine villa on the grounds of the royal palace. I insisted only that the house have a courtyard with a pond and blue lotus flowers. When Pharaoh traveled, he permitted Joseph to sit on his throne and conduct royal business.

Occasionally, I stood next to Joseph in the throne room as he heard petitions from the people. On one such day, two years into the famine, a palace servant asked permission to enter the throne room and speak. He bowed low in front of Joseph.

"Noble Zaphenath-paneah, 10 men from Canaan have arrived at the palace door and pleaded to make an appeal for food rations," the guard said. "They claim to be brothers and appear desperate and poor. They rode donkeys all the way from Canaan, I suspect, because they could not afford camels."

"Show them into the throne room," Joseph said. "I know how desperation feels."

As soon as the tattered, dust-covered men entered the throne room, Joseph stiffened.

"My eyes must deceive me," Joseph whispered.

The men bowed before him.

"Where do you come from?" Joseph said harshly.

"From Canaan, to procure food," they replied sheepishly.

"You are spies," Joseph called out loudly.

I had never heard such anger in Joseph's voice. I whispered his name, but he ignored me.

"No, my lord. Truly, your servants have come to procure food," they answered fearfully. "We are all of us sons of the same man; we are honest men; your servants have never been spies!"

"No, you have come to see the land in its nakedness," Joseph responded boldly.

I looked at the men and saw pitiful peasants. I worried that Joseph was losing his mind.

"We, your servants, were 12 brothers, sons of a certain man in the land of Canaan; the youngest, however, is now with his father and the other is no more," said one of the eldest brothers.

"It is just as I have told you: You are spies!" Joseph said in a voice that filled the throne room. "You shall be put to the test. Unless your youngest brother comes here, by power of Pharaoh, you shall not depart from this place! Let one of you go and bring your brother, while the rest of you are imprisoned."

"Joseph, show some compassion," I whispered, but again he ignored me.

"Confine these men in the guardhouse for three days," he said. "Then, we will decide which one may return to Canaan."

The cupbearer, scribe, and guards looked curiously at Joseph, for he was known for his gentleness and compassion. They followed his orders and escorted the men out of the throne room.

Left alone with Joseph, I said in shock, "Those men were pathetic and hungry. I never question your judgment, but what possessed you to imprison them?"

Joseph just stared ahead. Finally, he said, "Asenath, those men are my brothers."

My mother nearly fainted when I told her the news. When she caught her breath, she asked just one question, "Did they say if my mother is still alive?"

"They mentioned your father but not your mother," I said putting my arm around her.

Three days later, my mother wore her finest attire and a noblewoman's wig. She stood next to me in the throne room when her brothers were brought in.

"I need to see them with my own eyes," she had told Joseph and me. Joseph again spoke harshly to his brothers, yet his fury had begun to subside. He thought about the pain that he would inflict on his elderly father if he imprisoned nine brothers and only freed one. So Joseph threatened to imprison only one brother while the other nine returned to Canaan to retrieve Benjamin, their remaining brother and bring him to Egypt.

After Joseph spoke, one brother turned to the others and said, trembling, "We are being punished on account of Joseph."

A second brother cried out, "We simply looked at his anguish and paid no heed as he pleaded with us."

Still another confessed, "That is why this distress has come upon us."

Finally, the one who seemed eldest said, "Did I not tell you, 'Do no wrong to the boy?' But you paid no attention."

Joseph stood up and turned his back on his brothers. Tears flowed from his eyes. He wiped his face dry and turned back to his brothers. He pulled one brother, who I later learned was Simeon, from the group. My mother flinched when Simeon stood next to her. "I will imprison him while you return to Canaan and get your youngest brother," Joseph declared.

A royal guard came forward and took Simeon away. When his brothers left the throne room, Joseph told the servants to fill their donkey bags with grain, coins, and provisions.

"I will not starve my own brothers," Joseph told me. "Besides, I know that my father and Benjamin also need food."

Several moons passed, and the brothers did not return to Egypt.

"I thought that perhaps my brothers had changed," Joseph said. "But they have left Simeon to rot in prison."

That year, the rainy season again did not come. The Nile River grew shallow, and the famine continued. Only the land of Egypt had food. The heat grew more intense every day. Manasseh and Ephraim begged my mother and me to take them to a swimming hole. We made plans with a chariot driver to take us to an oasis known for its underground spring. When we returned that evening, Joseph was waiting outside our home in the dark.

"Asenath and Dinah, our brothers returned today and brought Benjamin," Joseph said slowly. "When I last saw Benjamin, he was little older than a baby. It took all my willpower not to reveal myself to him. I dined with our brothers in our house. Of course, I released Simeon from prison and gave them rations."

"Have they left to return to Canaan?" asked my mother.

"They will begin their journey at the crack of dawn," Joseph said. "But I have put a plan into motion. I had the house steward place my silver goblet in Benjamin's donkey bag. The steward will overtake them tomorrow and accuse Benjamin of thievery. By the time the sun reaches it highest point, they will be forced to return to our home."

"What is your purpose for this scheme?" I asked.

"I need to know if my brothers will protect Benjamin, my mother's other son. Once I trust that my brothers have truly changed," answered Joseph, "I will declare my true identity"

"What about my mother and me?" I asked in confusion. "Should we reveal ourselves or maintain our guises?"

"That decision is yours," Joseph said.

My mother spoke with resolve, "On the day that our family left the village of Nahor, my mother, Leah, refused to wear her veil. She said to me, 'I will not leave covered up and hidden.' Like my mother, I will not cover myself up and hide from our brothers any longer."

Joseph held my hand and said, "Asenath, you do not need to reveal your identity. Our brothers do not even know that you exist. Almost everybody thinks of you as Egyptian. Only Mother Zuleika, Potiphar, and perhaps a few others even remember that you were adopted."

My mother added, "I fear that our brothers will see you only as Shechem's daughter. They might not be able to hurt you physically, but Simeon and Levi can be mean-spirited and vile."

I walked outside in the night air alone and sat in our courtyard. The blue lotus flowers had already disappeared under the surface of the pond. I told myself that they must feel safe under the water, unseen and small. I lifted my charm inscribed with God's name out of my tunic and held it in my hand.

I prayed, "God of Sarah and Abraham, please tell me what to do."

As Joseph planned, the steward brought his brothers to our house by midday. Feigning anger, Joseph retrieved his cup and threatened to enslave Benjamin. The brothers looked in disbelief and fear at Joseph. Then Judah stepped forward. He pleaded with Joseph for Benjamin's release, recounting all that had befallen him and his brothers. Judah grew more frantic as he spoke.

Finally, Judah cried out, "Please let me remain as a slave instead of our youngest brother. Let him return with his brothers. For how can I go back to my father unless Benjamin is with me?"

Joseph, with tears running down his face, commanded, "Everybody please leave the room! I wish only my wife, her nursemaid, and these 11 brothers to remain."

When the room was empty except for our family members, Joseph stared into the eyes of each one of his brothers. Some of the brothers looked down in shame. Simeon and Levi trembled in fear. Judah stared back intensely. Finally, Joseph stood up and cried out, "I am Joseph."

A gasp filled the room, and the brothers stood dumbfounded. I saw relief on Joseph's face, even through his tears.

"Do not be distressed or blame yourselves for selling me into slavery," he said, continuing to weep. "God had a purpose in sending me ahead of you to Egypt. I saved lives by interpreting dreams."

Benjamin stepped up onto the platform and hugged Joseph tightly. When Benjamin began to cry, Joseph wept even louder. Composing himself, he said, "Please wait to celebrate our reunion. Certainly, you want to meet my wife and her nursemaid."

My mother stepped forward and took off her black Egyptian wig. Again, the brothers gasped and murmured among themselves.

"It cannot be possible," said Simeon.

"But it is possible," said my mother firmly. "I am Dinah, your sister." My mother smiled at me and nodded.

Joseph put his arm on my shoulder and said, "Let me introduce my wife, Asenath."

"I am Asenath," I began. Taking a deep breath, I grasped my charm necklace and thought of the faith of my ancestors. "My mother is Dinah. My father was Shechem, but he was never my parent. I consider myself a daughter of Israel."

I looked at Simeon and Levi and saw their faces grow dark with memories. Before they could say or do anything, Judah ran forward and hugged my mother, lifting her off her feet.

"Our plan worked," he said in joy. "Those merchants brought you to Egypt and saved you. Your daughter is beautiful. A true daughter of Israel."

"Our mother, Leah?" my mother asked.

"I am so sorry to tell you that she is dead—but she died peacefully and was buried with Abraham and Sarah. She never forgot you," Judah answered. "Zilpah and Bilhah are alive, though."

My mother did not have time to mourn, because Reuben embraced her, followed by Issachar and Zebulan, and then more brothers. Soon only Simeon and Levi stood off to the side.

"All is forgiven," Joseph said to them. Simeon and Levi came forward and bowed tentatively and awkwardly before Joseph.

Joseph said to them, "You need not bow. You are my brothers, not my servants."

When Pharaoh learned that Joseph's family had arrived, he greeted them warmly. Pharaoh commanded the brothers to return to Canaan and bring their wives and children, along with Jacob, Bilhah, and Zilpah, to Egypt. He promised to give our family land known for its good pastures.

Less than one moon later, the 11 brothers returned with their families. I met many girls and women—some, like Bilhah and Zilpah, were old and arthritic; some, like Tamar, had smiled through much pain; and some were just babies with many journeys ahead of them. We shared our stories, and through them became sisters. Together, we were the daughters of Israel.

Asenath takes her golden charm and places it in Lilith's ark. She listens carefully and says, "I hear your voices; tell me your stories, tell me who you are, Daughters of Israel."

When she grows old, she passes Lilith's ark onto the next generation. Lilith's ark has been passed from generation to generation until today.

Epilogue

LILITH

Do not close my ark just yet.
You have listened to our voices and heard our stories.
We ask that you do not forget—
   Eve's choice to seek the unknown,
Sarah's impulse to laugh and rejoice,
Hagar's courage to no longer be alone,
Rebekah's faith that she heard God's voice,
Rachel and Leah's reconciliation,
Dinah's determination to survive,
Tamar's cunning—but pure—dedication,
Asenath's decision to allow her true self to thrive.
   I have one more request before you go:
What story will you tell?
What gift will you bestow?
Share it now before we say farewell.
   You are the next link in the chain of our tradition,
I will treasure your gift as a holy addition.
And, when you close my ark's lid in the end,
Remember to pass the ark on to a sister, rival, or friend.

DISCUSSION GUIDE

Lilith's Ark strives to create dialogue between young biblical women and today's teenage girls. This discussion guide is meant to encourage conversation and further exploration. It can be used in various settings, including book clubs, youth groups, religious school or day school classes, camp programs, and mother-daughter Rosh Hodesh groups.

Lilith's Ark addresses many sensitive issues. Members of your discussion group may have emotional responses to certain topics or reveal personal information. Agree to make your discussions confidential. Group members must trust that any personal thoughts or experiences will not be shared with others. Confidences should only be broken if you are concerned about somebody's health or safety.

OPENING EXERCISE

When each young biblical woman is introduced, the meaning of her name is explained. Have each member of your group introduce herself by sharing her Hebrew or English name and its meaning. The group members might also share in whose honor they were named.

QUESTIONS TO ASK FOR EVERY CHAPTER

1. What is the significance of the object placed in the ark? Is it a fitting symbol for the main character?

2. Is the main character similar to you or to somebody you know? Do you share personality traits, experiences, or opinions with her? Do you like the main character? If you met, would you be friends?

3. How does the main character change over the course of her story? How do her experiences affect her outlook, self-image, and personality?

CHAPTER 1: EVE

Symbolic Object: The Seeds of an Apple
Verses from Torah: Genesis 2:4–3:24

Discussion Themes
• Gender Roles
• Maturing Knowledge
• Choices and Consequences

Discussion Questions

1. Adam tells Eve that she was created to be his helper. How would you have responded to Adam? Have you ever been assigned a role based on your age or gender? Who assigned this role to you—a teacher, your parents, siblings, or friends? What challenges have you faced if you have wanted to break out of this role?

2. Eve chooses to pursue knowledge, even though Adam warns her that God forbids it. Why do you believe she made this choice? What does she hope to gain through eating from the Tree of Knowledge?

3. The serpent shows Eve the potential for knowledge. Do you view the serpent as a positive or negative character?

4. Eve eats from the Tree of Knowledge first and thus matures before Adam. In your experience, do girls tend to mature before boys? If so, what difficulties can this create?

5. Eve blames the serpent rather than taking responsibility for breaking God's rules. Have you ever "blamed the serpent"?

6. Does Eve and Adam's punishment fit their disobedience? Do you think Eve would have broken God's rule if she had known the consequences? Think about a time when you broke a rule and were punished. Was your disobedience worth the punishment?

Extending the Exploration

1. Traditional Jewish law assigns distinct roles to women and men. Investigate and discuss traditional Jewish gender roles. How have these roles evolved in recent generations?

2. Judaism and Christianity have very different approaches to Eve and Adam eating from the Tree of Knowledge. Investigate the Christian interpretation. How does it differ from the Jewish interpretation?

A Mother and Daughter Dialogue

Gender roles have changed dramatically over the past several generations. Talk with your mother about expectations, roles, and challenges for girls when she was young. How do they compare to today? Expand the conversation by asking the same questions of your grandmother or another woman of her generation.

CHAPTER 2: SARAH

Symbolic Object: The Map

Verses from Torah: Genesis 11:24–12:9, 16:1–18:15, 21:1–13, 25:1

Discussion Themes

• Evolving Relationships with Parents
• Dreams for the Future
• Jealousy

Discussion Questions

1. How does Sarah envision her adult life? What dreams does she hold? Do you have specific expectations and hopes for your future? How do your expectations compare with Sarah's?

2. Sarah must modify her dreams to meet life's circumstances. She takes on roles that she never imagined for herself. How do her dreams change? Does she mourn her lost dreams? Have you ever had a dream that could not be realized? What emotions did you face? How did you modify your dream in response? Have you ever taken on a role, responsibility, or task that you never imagined for yourself?

3. Sarah paints a vivid picture of life for a young woman in biblical times. How does her world compare to yours? What are the greatest differences? Are there any similarities?

4. Sarah resists leaving home to marry. Do you sympathize with Sarah? How do you feel about gaining more independence from your parents? Do your parents resist your growing independence? If so, how have you confronted this conflict?

5. Why do you believe that Sarah became so jealous of Hagar? Were you angry with or sympathetic to Sarah? Has jealousy or competition ever had an impact on your relationships and friendships?

6. Sarah almost immediately regrets asking Hagar to have a baby for her. Have you ever made a decision or put a plan into motion that you regretted afterward?

7. Why was laughter significant to Sarah? Does laughter aid our ability to reach goals or fulfill dreams? Do you remember a time in your life when laughter helped you to overcome a challenge or confront an emotional situation?

Extending the Exploration

1. Sarah travels great distances in her life. Her map serves as her guide. Talk to the women in your family. Where have they lived? What journeys have they made? How did their different homes influence their lives? Create a map detailing the journeys of the women in your family.

2. Read the story of the *Akedah*, the Binding of Isaac, in Genesis 22. Sarah dies at the beginning of the next chapter. In their *midrashim*, the ancient rabbis said Sarah dies from shock and grief when she learns that Abraham nearly sacrificed Isaac. Create your own *midrash* describing Sarah's reaction to the *Akedah*.

A Mother and Daughter Dialogue

As Sarah grows older, she must separate from her parents. She finds this change difficult and misses her mother tremendously. Ask your mother about how her relationship with your grandparents evolved over time. As a teenager, what conflicts did she face with her parents? Are they similar to or different from conflicts that you and your mother have had with one another? How did she feel when she moved out of her parents' house?

CHAPTER 3: HAGAR

Symbolic Object: The Blanket
Verses from Torah: Genesis 16:1–16, 17:15–22, 21:9–21, 25:1

Discussion Themes

• Surviving Difficult Circumstances
• Family Dynamics
• Trust in Other People and in Ourselves

Discussion Questions

1. Hagar makes difficult and perhaps unconventional decisions. She chooses to leave her home to become a slave and, later, to have a baby for Sarah. Why does she make these decisions? Does she have other choices? Have you ever made an unconventional or unexpected choice for yourself?

2. Hagar survives poverty, slavery, and abandonment. What coping mechanisms does she create for herself? Are these methods effective and healthy? Recall a challenging time in your own life. What coping mechanisms did you create for yourself?

3. Why does Hagar have difficulty trusting other people? How do you know if you can trust another person? Whom do you trust when you need support?

4. Hagar faces complex family dynamics both in her birth family and in her relationship with Sarah and Abraham. How do birth order, poverty, and her father's disability affect Hagar's birth family? How do jealousy, Hagar's role as a servant, and distrust affect her relationship with Sarah and Abraham? What factors affect the dynamics of your own family?

5. Hagar and Sarah tell the same story from different perspectives. How do their recollections of and assumptions about each other differ?

6. At the end of the story, Hagar becomes desperate and wants to give up. What gives her the will and ability to survive? Have you ever faced a situation so challenging or upsetting that you wanted to give up? Who or what gave you the will to persevere?

7. At moments of deepest despair, Hagar hears from God. Do you believe that God supports us through difficult times? Has your faith supported you through challenges?

Extending the Exploration

1. When Sarah faces infertility, Hagar becomes a surrogate mother to provide Sarah and Abraham with an heir. Investigate what modern Judaism says about infertility treatments and surrogate motherhood.

2. With Hagar's desperation in mind, research the resources for young people facing desperation and depression in your own community. Invite a social worker or psychologist to talk about how to help a friend in emotional need.

A Mother and Daughter Dialogue

Ask your mother about her sense of faith. Does she believe God reaches out to individuals at times of need? Have her spirituality, faith, or religious convictions helped her through difficult times? When has she felt closest to God or religion? Has she ever questioned her faith? Do you hold similar spiritual beliefs?

CHAPTER 4: REBEKAH

Symbolic Object: The Water Jug
Verses from Torah: Genesis 24:1–67

Discussion Themes

• Spirituality
• Fate and Callings
• Taking Risks and Facing Disappointments

Discussion Questions

1. Rebekah has faith that she hears God speaking to her. Do you believe that God speaks to individuals? Why do you think some people have a stronger spiritual connection than others? What have been spiritual moments in your life?

2. Rebekah describes a feeling of serenity when she hears from God. Where does this serenity come from? Have you ever experienced such a serene moment?

3. Rebekah's friends and family don't believe that God has spoken to her. Why do they find it so difficult to believe Rebekah? If one of your friends

said that God spoke to her, how would you react? Why do you think that society stigmatizes people who say that God has spoken to them?

4. Deborah, Rebekah's nursemaid, supports Rebekah when others do not. How does Rebekah's relationship with Deborah differ from her relationship with her mother and grandmother? Do you have a "Deborah" in your life—a woman other than your mother whom you trust and can confide in?

5. Fate is an important aspect of Rebekah's story. Do you believe that our lives are "fated"? If so, why do our individual decisions and actions matter?

6. What does Rebekah mean by her "calling"? How does her calling change throughout the story? Do you feel that you have or will have a calling in life?

7. Rebekah enjoys her friendship with Adinah yet sometimes wants solitude. Do you enjoy being alone? How do you tell your friends that you need some space?

8. Rebekah takes a risk to follow her dream. Would you have been able to take such a risk? What gave her the courage? This dream is shattered when Deborah tells her about the *Akedah* and Sarah's death. How does she react to this disappointment and overcome it?

Extending the Exploration

1. Read the story of Hannah in the first chapter of I Samuel. Hannah, like Rebekah, is a woman with great faith. She is a role model in Judaism for the power of prayer. Her story is so important in our tradition that it is the Haftarah for the first day of Rosh Hashanah. Compare Hannah's and Rebekah's sense of spirituality, assertiveness, and willingness for self-sacrifice.

2. Rebekah's family blesses her when she leaves home with Eliezer. Put yourself in the position of Rebekah's family and write your own blessing for her departure.

A Mother and Daughter Dialogue

Rebekah's mother dismisses her beliefs as simply a teen "vision of grandeur." What might have prompted such disbelief? Do teenagers often have "visions of grandeur" that fade away? How did your mother imagine her future when she was a young woman? Has she realized any part of this vision?

CHAPTER 5: RACHEL

Symbolic Object: The Idols
Verses from Torah: Genesis 29:1–31:21

Discussion Themes

• Body Image
• Sibling Rivalry
• Attraction and Compatibility

Discussion Questions

1. Rachel and Leah are very different from one another. Do they acknowledge their differences? Are they sympathetic to the challenges that the other sister faces? How are you different from your siblings? Have you ever viewed a sibling as a rival?

2. Rachel overhears her parents talking about being unable to find a husband for Leah. She chooses not to tell her sister what she overhears. Do you agree with Rachel's choice? Have you ever withheld information to protect another person's feelings?

3. How does Rachel feel about her appearance? How does her beauty affect how other people interact with her? Do you feel that you are judged on your appearance? Do you think it is difficult to be "too beautiful"?

4. Rachel confides in her mother that she feels uncomfortable when the shepherd boys call her "Asherah" and the tax collector leers at her. Her mother responds: "You should thank the gods for having such a problem." Have you ever confided in somebody who reacted by minimizing your feelings?

5. The medicine woman Rafaela says that Leah's deformed eyes are a punishment. That night, Leah asks, "Rachel, what is my sin?" How would you answer Leah's question? Do you feel that unfortunate events are punishment for wrongdoing?

6. Jacob is immediately drawn to Rachel. Why does Rachel not return his affection? Is his attraction based solely on her appearance? What attracts two people to one another?

7. Rachel suggests that Leah marry Jacob. She believes that both she and Leah will benefit. Her plot goes terribly wrong. What factors did Rachel and Leah not consider? Have you ever tried to do something good only for it to have negative consequences?

8. Rachel and Leah are close as young girls, yet when they reach young adulthood, their relationship becomes strained. How do childhood friendships change over time? Do you have childhood friends from whom you have drifted apart? Why?

Extending the Exploration

1. The shepherd boys' flirtations and the tax collector's roaming eyes make Rachel feel immodest. *Tzeniut*, or "modesty," is a Jewish value. Research what traditional Judaism teaches about *tzeniut*. What do you consider immodest? How might the value of *tzeniut* apply to your choices in dress, speech, and behavior? Is it difficult to be modest in today's world?

2. Bilhah and Zilpah undoubtedly have their own stories to tell. Create your own *midrash* written from one of their viewpoints.

A Mother and Daughter Dialogue

Rachel's young adult years are shaped largely by her relationships with her sister and mother. Ask your mother about the girls and women who shaped her adolescence. What did she learn from them? How did her relationships with these women evolve as she grew older?

CHAPTER 6: LEAH

Symbolic Object: A Root of a Mandrake
Verses from Torah: Genesis 29:1–31:16

Discussion Themes

• Coping with a Disability
• Types of Love
• Reconciliation

Discussion Questions

1. Leah and Rachel tell essentially the same story from two different points of view. How do their recollections contrast with one another? Do you think that Leah and Rachel would be surprised if they heard one another's perspectives?

2. Leah struggles with a disability that restricts her freedom and isolates her socially. How does she cope with this disability? What skills and strengths does she develop because of her disability? Do you or does somebody in your family have a disability? What are the effects of this disability on you and your family?

3. Leah's cousins taunt her and spread rumors about her. How does Leah react to this name-calling? Did she have options to make the taunts stop? Have you ever been the victim of teasing or bullying? How did you respond?

4. Leah prides herself on her intelligence and medical discoveries. But men consider her a medicine woman, not a potential wife. Do you think it is difficult for smart girls, especially those talented in the sciences, to feel or be attractive to boys? Do girls ever hide their intelligence?

5. Leah loves Jacob, yet her affection is not returned. How does this rejection affect her? Should Leah have continued to pursue Jacob despite his lack of feelings for her? If a person is attracted to you and you are not interested, how should you react?

6. Jacob tells Leah: "I do love you, Leah. I just love Rachel differently." What do you think he means? Can love take different forms? If you were Leah, how would you respond to Jacob's statement?

7. Leah and Rachel are estranged for many years. Are they equally to blame for this estrangement? How might they have healed their relationship sooner? Have you ever had a falling-out with a friend? Were you able to heal your friendship?

8. How do Leah and Rachel switch roles as the fortunate and unfortunate one, as their story progresses? How does this reversal of fortune help them reconcile with one another?

9. If Jacob had not entered their lives, do you think that Leah's and Rachel's relationship would still have been strained? How does Jacob's treatment of

Leah and Rachel contribute to the tension between them? Have you ever had the experience of a boy coming between you and a friend? How can a girl protect her friendships while developing a romantic relationship?

Expanding the Exploration

1. Leviticus 19:14 states, "You shall not insult the deaf, or place a stumbling block before the blind...." From this verse, we learn about the mitzvah of *lo titein michshol* or meeting the needs of the disabled. Study more about this mitzvah and how our contemporary Jewish community helps the disabled.

2. Leah's cousins spread rumors and taunt her. Rafaela's insensitive prayer gives Leah nightmares. *Lashon ha-ra'* means "evil speech" or "gossip." Our tradition teaches that our words have great power and we should choose them carefully. Study the mitzvah of refraining from *lashon ha-ra'* and discuss its relevance for today.

A Mother and Daughter Dialogue

Rejection or unrequited love hurts nearly every person at some point in her life. Discuss Leah's predicament with your mother. Can your mother sympathize with Leah? Did your mother ever face rejection? How did she heal her emotional wounds?

CHAPTER 7: DINAH

Symbolic Object: The Painted Jacket
Verses from Torah: Genesis 31:19–34:31

A Note of Caution

Acquaintance rape is a particularly sensitive and difficult topic. It is natural for Dinah's story to upset you. Be open with your feelings, reactions, and questions. *Lilith's Ark* is intended for readers with ranging ages; depending on the age and interests of your group, you may choose not to discuss some of themes in this chapter or questions suggested below. It is strongly advised to include at least one trusted adult in your discussion of this chapter. You might also consider inviting a trained professional to facilitate this discussion. Your rabbi, a rape crisis center, a guidance counselor, or Jewish Children and Family Services should be able to recommend a facilitator. If you cannot arrange for a facilitator, have the phone number and literature from a local rape crisis center available.

Discussion Themes

• Acquaintance Rape
• Meeting Parental Expectations
• Cycle of Violence

Discussion Questions

1. Dinah is one of the youngest children and the only daughter in a family of many boys. How does being the baby sister to so many brothers influence her identity and actions? What is the birth order in your family? If you have siblings, how have they influenced you?

2. Jacob expects Dinah to be passive and refined. Dinah struggles to fulfill her father's expectations. Do you find yourself trying to live up to your parents' expectations? What happens when their expectations conflict with your own?

3. Dinah and Shechem's relationship builds up to rape. What were the warning signs? Why did Dinah have a hard time asking for help? If Dinah had confided in you about Shechem's increasing possessiveness and unwanted advances, what would you have said?

4. Dinah struggles to survive emotionally after Shechem rapes her. What helps Dinah be a survivor and not a victim? How does Alit help her recover?

5. Simeon and Levi's revenge on the city of Shechem is brutal. Do you think Simeon's and Levi's retribution for Dinah's rape was justified? Where did their rage come from? How can a cycle of violence be broken?

Expanding the Exploration

1. Acquaintance rape or date rape accounts for more than 50% of all rapes and up to 90% of rapes involving adolescents. Invite a social worker, perhaps from a rape crisis center, to facilitate a discussion about this sensitive and important subject. Learn the warning signs of a relationship prone to violence, skills for protecting yourself, and where in your community to ask for help.

2. Rebekah visits Dinah and her family at Rosh Hodesh, the new moon. Jewish women often gather at Rosh Hodesh for study, celebration, and

prayer. Investigate women's celebrations on Rosh Hodesh and hold a Rosh Hodesh gathering of your own.

A Mother and Daughter Dialogue

When Shechem begins acting aggressively toward Dinah, she does not confide in her mother. Why not? Why is it sometimes difficult for girls to talk to their mothers?

CHAPTER 8: TAMAR

Symbolic Object: The Copper Mirror
Verses from Torah: Genesis 38:1–30

Discussion Themes

• Disguising Our Identity
• Love and Loyalty
• Personal Values

Discussion Questions

1. Tamar wears several different types of outfits: costumes as an actress, fine clothing for her betrothal and wedding, widow's garb, and a harlot's costume. How does Tamar feel in each outfit? How does her identity change with each outfit? Do you ever wear "costumes" that "mask" your true identity? Have you seen other girls do this?

2. Tamar and Er are immediately drawn to one another and quickly fall in love. Do you believe in love at first sight? After Tamar and Er's first attraction to one another, do other factors contribute to their relationship's strength?

3. Tamar maintains her loyalty to Er for years after his death. Do you find her loyalty admirable or obsessive? What contributes to loyalty in a relationship, and what are its bounds?

4. Judah believes Tamar brings a curse upon his family. He breaks his promise and avoids allowing her to marry Shelah. Do you sympathize with Judah? Do you believe in curses? Have you ever felt cursed?

5. Do you approve of Tamar's accepting the role of a harlot? Did she have other options? Do you think that she was motivated more by her loyalty to Er, her desire to no longer be a childless widow, or her anger at Judah for breaking his promise to her?

6. By accepting the role of a harlot, Tamar challenges her values, the rules of morality by which she lives. What are your most important personal values? Can you imagine an instance when you might break them?

Expanding the Exploration

1. Read Ruth 4:18–22, the genealogy of Perez to King David. Do you find it odd or troubling that King David descends from the union of Tamar and Judah? Or do you find it refreshing that King David's lineage is not particularly noble? For further exploration, study 2 Samuel 7:12–16. These verses form the foundation of the belief that the Messiah will descend from King David.

2. As girls and women, we have complex identities and wear many "guises" in our different roles. Purchase a plain face mask or cut a mask out of cardboard. Clip pictures from magazines to symbolize different aspects of your identity. Create a collage with these pictures on your mask.

A Mother and Daughter Dialogue

Zachor, the injunction to remember and honor the dead, is an important Jewish value. Talk to your mother about a relative or a friend who has died. What does she miss the most about this person? How does she keep this person's memory alive?

CHAPTER 9: ASENATH

Symbolic Object: The Golden Necklace
Verses from Torah: Genesis 39:1–46:8

Discussion Themes

• Religious and Ethnic Identity
• Mother and Daughter Relationships
• Courage

Discussion Questions

1. Asenath considers herself both Egyptian and a daughter of Israel. What conflicts arise from her dual identity? What does she gain from each aspect of her identity? How do you merge your Jewish identity with your secular identity? Do conflicts ever arise?

2. In public, Asenath hides her identity as a daughter of Israel. Why is she not more forthcoming? Were you angry at Asenath for hiding her identity? What do you think gives her the courage finally to reveal her identity? Have you ever hidden your Jewish identity or another aspect of your background?

3. Joseph explains his dual identity to Asenath: "Although I appear Egyptian, I feel like a son of Israel. I pray out loud to Egyptian gods and silently to the God of Sarah and Abraham." How does acknowledging their similar struggles bring Asenath and Joseph closer to one another?

4. Asenath and Joseph are first friends and then gradually fall in love. What steps do they take to establish their relationship? How does the gradual growth of their relationship add to its strength? How do you imagine the process of falling in love and developing a committed relationship?

5. Both Dinah and Mother Zuleika are supportive of Asenath, but in different ways. Describe Dinah's and Mother Zuleika's parenting styles. What does Asenath gain from her relationship with each mother?

6. How did you react when Asenath called Dinah her confidante and closest friend? Do you consider your mother to be a friend?

7. Asenath and Mother Zuleika have a strained relationship. What factors contribute to this discord? Does Mother Zuleika place more pressure on Asenath than a typical parent? Do you think Mother Zuleika loves Asenath?

8. Do you view Mother Zuleika as positive or negative? Can a negative relationship have positive aspects?

9. Both Dinah and Asenath exhibit courage when they reveal their true identities. What fears do they need to confront? What gives them the strength for such courage?

10. Asenath concludes her story by calling herself a daughter of Israel. What does it mean to Asenath to be a daughter of Israel? What does it mean to you?

Expand the Exploration

1. During the Spanish Inquisition, many Jews became Marranos to escape persecution. A Marrano was a convert to Catholicism who practiced Judaism secretly. Some descendants of Marranos maintained their culture until modern times. Research the history and customs of Marranos. How are Asenath, Dinah, and Joseph similar to the Marranos?

2. At the end of her story, Asenath meets Tamar. The two women are roughly the same age. Imagine a conversation between Asenath and Tamar and write your own *midrash* describing it. Consider expanding your *midrash* by having Dinah meet Tamar as well.

A Mother and Daughter Dialogue

Zuleika presses Asenath to study hard, perfect her appearance, and learn social graces. Does Zuleika expect too much from Asenath? What are the consequences, both positive and negative, of such expectations? What are your mother's expectations for you? Do you ever feel pressured by her expectations or the expectations of others?

CONCLUDING EXERCISES

1. At the end of the epilogue, Lilith tells the reader to place an item in the ark and pass the ark onto another young woman. What item would you place in Lilith's ark? To whom would you pass the ark after you?

2. Think about the young women of Genesis. With whom do you most identify? Whom do you most admire? If you could meet only one of the women, whom would you choose?